The GUTSY GIRL

ESCAPADES for YOUR LIFE of EPIC ADVENTURE

CAROLINE PAUL

illustrated by WENDY MACNAUGHTON

BLOOMSBURY

NEW YORK · LONDON · OXFORD · NEW DELHI · SYDNEY

Bloomsbury USA
An imprint of Bloomsbury Publishing Plc

50 Bedford Square   1385 Broadway
London, WC1B 3DP   New York, NY 10018
UK   USA

www.bloomsbury.com
BLOOMSBURY and the Diana logo are trademarks of Bloomsbury Publishing Plc

First published 2016

Text © Caroline Paul 2016
Illustrations © Wendy MacNaughton 2016

ISBN: HB: 978-1-63286-123-8
ePub: 978-1-63286-124-5

LIBRARY OF CONGRESS CATALOGING-IN-PUBLICATION DATA

Paul, Caroline. MacNaughton, Wendy, illustrator.
The gutsy girl : escapades for your life of epic adventure /
Caroline Paul ; illustrations by Wendy MacNaughton.
pages cm
ISBN 978-1-63286-123-8 (hardback) ISBN 978-1-63286-124-5 (ebook)
Paul, Caroline—Juvenile literature. Adventure and adventurers—Juvenile literature.
Women adventurers—Juvenile literature. Confidence—Juvenile literature. Risk-taking
(Psychology)—Juvenile literature. JUVENILE NONFICTION / Games & Activities / General. JUVENILE
NONFICTION Girls & Women. FAMILY & RELATIONSHIPS / Parenting / General.
G525 .P3767 2016
DDC 910.4092—dc23
2015020030

4 6 8 10 9 7 5

Designed and typeset by Elizabeth Van Itallie

Printed and bound by CPI Group (UK) Ltd, Croydon, CR0 4YY

To find out more about our authors and books visit www.bloomsbury.com. Here you will find extracts, author interviews, details of forthcoming events and the option to sign up for our newsletters.

Bloomsbury books may be purchased for business or promotional use. For information on bulk purchases please contact Macmillan Corporate and Premium Sales Department at specialmarkets@macmillan.com.

A SHORT NOTE FROM THE AUTHOR

Dear Gutsy Girl,

I HAVE BEEN politely asked by my lawyers and my insurance company to remind you that I have had many adventures in my life that were perfectly planned, well executed, and hazard free.

But let's face it, uneventful trips are boring. None of those adventures is in this book.

Instead, I have willfully chosen to write about the few that ended in mishap and mayhem—thus frightening your parents, alerting your local hospital, and gluing you to these pages—because it is in those moments that I learned the most essential lessons: how to be brave, how to persevere, how to stay focused, how to laugh at myself, and more.

I am not suggesting you get yourself into the many pickles that I describe here. But the lessons are a gift from me to you. From them I hope you learn not how to avoid every hairball situation, but how to navigate your way through them, because challenging yourself is essential to a gutsy girl's life of exhilaration, self-confidence, and fun.

Enough talk! Begin the book! And don't forget to read the warning at the beginning very carefully. After that, enjoy the ensuing pages. Then swan dive with exuberance into adventures of your own.

Caroline Paul

(The Author)

To all the Gutsy Girls
who were cautioned
that they shouldn't, wouldn't, or couldn't . . .
and they did.
Thank you.

CONTENTS

SOME RELEVANT DEFINITIONS

Gutsy

1. Having a great deal of nerve or courage
2. Having lots of intestines and stuff

Derring-do

Brave acts; behavior that requires courage; daring action
(from the Middle English "dorring don," which means "daring to do,"
first used in 1579. Often used with words like swashbuckling, kickass,
WOW!, and, of course, gutsy.)

Adventure

1. (NOUN) An exciting or remarkable experience
2. (VERB) To proceed despite risk. "She decided to adventure into the
wilderness, because she had loads of backpacking experience, bear-proof
food cans, chocolate, a really good map, an even better head on her
shoulders, an emergency kit, an A- on her school report on edible plants,
and, of course, a gutsy disposition."

CHAPTER 1

DREAM BIG, MAKE IT REAL

WHEN I WAS thirteen, I read about a strange boat race. The boats were elaborate affairs—paddlewheels, schooners, rowboats—with one thing in common. They were kept afloat by milk cartons.

I wasn't a sailor. I wasn't a milk carton fanatic. But for some reason I loved this idea. I wanted to build a milk carton boat. Specifically a milk carton pirate ship. I envisioned a three-masted vessel, with a plank off to one side (of course) and a huge curved prow that ended in an eagle head. So I set about collecting milk cartons. I collected from my school cafeteria. I collected from my friends. I collected from my family. I soon became familiar with the look on their faces when I explained I was building a milk carton pirate ship. It was actually a combination of looks, all rolled into one. *Hahaha, what a crazy idea*, the expression said. And, *Good luck, kid, but I don't think it's going to happen.* And, *Well, at least I'm getting rid of my milk cartons.* Then at the very end of this facial conga dance, I always caught something else. *Actually, that sounds like FUN. I wish I could do that*, the final look exclaimed.

You can do it, I should have said back. But it's hard to contradict the large cafeteria cook who smells of sliced ham and oatmeal. I didn't say anything. But I understood the feeling.

I had been a shy and fearful kid. Many things had scared me. Bigger kids. Second grade. The elderly woman across the street. Being called on in class. The book *Where the Wild Things Are.* Woods at dusk. The way the bones in my hand crisscrossed.

Being scared was a terrible feeling, like sinking in quicksand. My stomach would drop, my feet would feel heavy, my head would prickle. Fear was an all-body experience. For a shy kid like me it was overwhelming.

Now I wanted to build a milk carton pirate ship and sail it along a body of water. Did I mention that I didn't know how to sail? And I use the term "sail" loosely. I really mean "get pulled by the current to my destination." I didn't even know how to do that.

GIRL HERO!

Laura Dekker was a month shy of fifteen when she set sail in 2010 on Guppy, a boat she and her father remodeled together. Her goal? To become the youngest to circumnavigate the globe alone.

Naysayers, and even the Dutch courts, tried to intervene, claiming that she was too young. She sailed anyway, stopping off at islands and ports, expertly navigating storms and wild seas.

A year and a half later, she had successfully circumnavigated the world. And you know what? She kept sailing. Today she lives aboard *Guppy*, her adventures continuing.

SHE SAID...

"Adventure is worthwhile in itself." —**Amelia Earhart**, pilot

What had happened to the shy and fearful kid?

She was still there. But somewhere along the way I had decided that she wasn't having a lot of fun. I wanted a life of Grand Adventure, the kind I had read about in books. So I started to kindly tell the shy and fearful girl to step back, and make way for the adventurous girl that was also there. The girl who really wanted to captain a milk carton pirate ship.

Where does a boat-builder keep her materials? Under her bed, of course. Within a month I had a bunch of milk cartons. Within two months I had more. Within three months a strange smell took hold. It hadn't occurred to me that I had to rinse anything out! Within four months I was the proud owner of 167 (now clean) milk cartons. I was ready.

I taped the tops of all the milk cartons closed. I bound them in groups of three and wrapped each group in a garbage bag. I taped the garbage bag closed and then wrapped it in another garbage bag. I didn't know much about buoyancy, but I did know that as long as I kept the water out, the milk cartons would float—like any intelligent boat-builder, I had tested this before I began. But that's where my intelligence ended. Because I had overlooked one crucial element: I wasn't adept at building anything; I wasn't handy. More importantly my dad wasn't handy.

My dad was game, though. He didn't laugh when I told him my plan. Well, he chuckled a little, sure. But he liked the idea. He appreciated weird ideas, I found out later. He liked acupuncture before it became an accepted medical procedure. He believed in psychics. He thought that talking to animals was possible, if you put your mind to it. My dad himself was not weird. He was a banker who wore ties and shiny leather shoes to work and had one martini

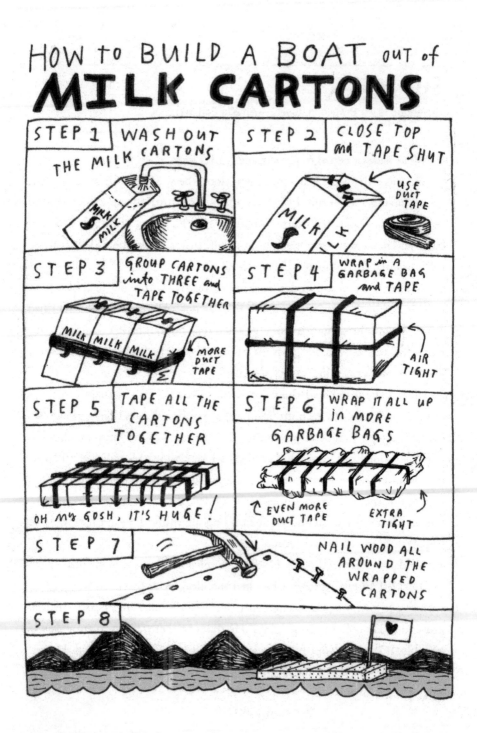

GIRL HEROES!

Rafting the Grand Canyon's big waters is exciting enough, but how about running all three hundred miles of its monster waves and sucking holes on a boogie board? **Julie Munger**, **Kelley Kalafatich**, and **Rebecca Rusch** donned wetsuits and fins and, towing their own supplies for nineteen days in November 2001, became the first to "river board" this mighty stretch of white water.

when he came home. But at the time I didn't know that he liked the milk carton pirate ship idea because it was weird. I thought he liked it because it was cool. He let me think that, too. I'm not sure it would have mattered if I had known. I was crazy about my dad, and building a boat with him meant that we would spend time together. It felt like a crucial part of the adventure.

I didn't know how to build a boat, he didn't know how to build a boat. Somehow I thought that meant a boat would be built, as if the empty parts of our mind where boat-building knowledge was supposed to lie was now so huge it would automatically vacuum in the information. Unfortunately, this was not so.

A pirate ship quickly became out of the question. Paddlewheel? Nope. Rowboat? Nah. My dad and I settled on what most people would call a "square." We called it a "raft." We stacked the milk cartons onto a piece of plywood about the size of a double bed. We lay another piece of plywood on top. We hammered planks of wood along each side. It took about fifteen nails in all. I named it the HMS *Homogenized*. It was beautiful.

I invited my sister, Alexandra, on the maiden voyage, which would take place on the local river. My sister and I were like any other pair of sisters: We fought, we shared clothes, sometimes we told on each other, sometimes we kept each other's secrets, we laughed together to the point of hiccups and

SHE SAID...

"I've worked too hard and too long to let anything stand in the way of my goals. I will not let my teammates down and I will not let myself down." —**Mia Hamm**, super-duper soccer player

stomach muscles strains, we cried easily in the other's presence. Unlike most sisters, we were born on the same day, two minutes apart. We were twins.

We looked enough alike that people called us The Girls, as if we were one entity without separate names. But we didn't look exactly alike, which meant that people often compared us, too. Being compared felt like being scrutinized for the lead in a school play, constantly. Who would get her name in lights? Who would get attention? For these reasons I didn't love being a twin at the time (as a grown-up, I love it.) But being a twin contributed to my pirate ship bravado. I was determined to distinguish myself from my sister. Once the boat was built, I wouldn't merely be part of The Girls. I would be a captain. Of a square. Made of milk cartons. Try to top that, World.

I offered my twin the lofty position of first mate. I didn't know exactly what a first mate did, and she didn't either, but she agreed anyway. She asked some technical questions, like how the raft was going to move.

It was a good question. The three-masted sail of my original plan was nowhere in sight.

"Canoe paddles," I said.

"Okay," she said, satisfied.

You would think she would've asked a few more questions. But she trusted me, just as I trusted her. No matter how much we fought, or cried, or tried to distance ourselves from the other, we had a deep connection that came from being made of the same genetic material. I would follow her anywhere. She would follow me anywhere. Even if it was stupid. Even if it was down the local river.

I had never paid much attention to the local river—we preferred to play and swim in the local lake. This was why I didn't know that the local river was the site of many high-caliber kayak races. That wouldn't have stopped me, of course. Anyway, the river was very low, and it looked easy to navigate on a wooden raft (square) filled with 167 milk cartons.

This is how it must have looked to my parents, too, who said nothing about any possible danger. They were good parents, but not good river assessors.

My twin designed a flag. She wrote "HMS Homogenized" on a white bed sheet, and tied it to a long stick. This was a sorry excuse for a flag. It looked more like a bed sheet tied to a long stick than anything else, but we didn't care. We had a boat, we had canoe paddles, we had a sort-of flag—and soon we had a crew. Our friend Charlie agreed to join, as did a local French exchange student named Marianne. I wore tube socks, which were all the rage at the time, and matching sweat bands on my head and wrists, as if I knew there would be a lot of hard, sweaty sailing work ahead. We took an oath of loyalty, and we sang a few sea shanties. Then we pushed off.

Ahead of us was a few hundred feet of flat water. This would be quickly followed by a set of rapids. Charlie and Alexandra and Marianne eyed the rapids with suspicion. But these rapids looked far away and pretty small. In fact, they

GIRL HERO!

Ka'iulani Murphy is an ocean navigator. But she doesn't use modern equipment like GPS, radar, or even a compass. Instead she navigates according to ancient wayfinding techniques. These include pinpointing stars and planets, understanding currents, winds, and the flight patterns of birds, deciphering cloud formations, and reading wave direction. It is believed that this is how Ka'iulani's Hawaiian ancestors navigated the arduous route from Asia to the Polynesian islands on large voyaging canoes more than a thousand years ago. Today Ka'iulani guides a replica of that ancient sailing vessel, called the Hokule'a, on a four-year journey around the world.

were small *because* they were far away. It's called "an optical illusion." It's also called "denial."

We could have started below the rapids, and then enjoyed a few miles of flat water, but this seemed to be cheating. We had a boat, a flag, a crew, an oath, and some sea shanties; surely we could handle some rapids.

Turns out we didn't need rapids to begin our descent from "adventure" to "misadventure." The HMS *Homogenized* went out of control almost immediately. This may have been because it was a square, which was not very hydrodynamic. It also may have been that the four kids on it had no idea what they were doing. The raft spun like a carnival ride in the swift water, and as it did my crew began to laugh hysterically. As captain I told them that this counted as mutinous behavior, grounds for walking the plank and whatnot. But I was laughing too (and we didn't have a plank, anyway). We were desperately out of control and we hadn't even reached the rapids yet.

There was a loud roar. Or that was what it sounded like to ears that were already losing their equilibrium. It was actually sort of a medium-size roar, from medium-size rapids. Still, if you heard a roar from a lion, would you feel better if someone said, "Don't worry, that lion is only medium-size"?

Exactly.

We dropped into the first rapid. There may or may not have been some pitiful screaming. Marianne may have yelled, *"Zut, alors!"* My twin might have reconsidered her trust in me. Mostly, though, there was still laughing.

SHE SAID...

"There's no such thing as bad weather. There's just not enough clothes."
—**Julie Munger**, white-water rafter and pioneering river boarder, on braving frigid water temperatures and winter rains during the first descent of the Grand Canyon on a river board.

We were a brave bunch of sailors. Then there was a loud crack. A rock ripped our underside. One of the fifteen nails popped. Another five gave way. Milk cartons wrapped in garbage bags began to float down the river.

Charlie and Marianne and I scrambled and belly-flopped to shore. The only one who hung on was the first mate, my twin. She made it past the rapids on a badly lilting raft, which was now quickly becoming a sad, sinking square. The final nine nails gave way. The first mate abandoned ship, gripping our flag.

"Abandon ship!" I yelled, because I could think of nothing else to say.

"I already have!" the first mate yelled back in a mutinous sort of way. Then she waved the flag to indicate she was okay.

Our grand adventure had been cut very short. It was a sad, sad end to months of preparation and hope. On the other hand I had commanded a ship that I had fashioned with my own hands (with a lot of help from my dad), a ship that I had dreamed about and then made real. Okay, so it wasn't a pirate ship. It was a square. But it was a square that had a crew, a sort-of-flag, an oath, a few sea shanties, and a (short) wild river ride to its name. How cool is that?

DERRING-DO
CONNECT WITH SOMEONE NEW

Joining a sports team or a milk carton expedition? First impressions matter! Don't wait for someone to say hello—introduce yourself first in these three simple steps!

1. Look the person in the eye.

2. Speak clearly and state your name. "Hi, my name is Caroline. It's nice to meet you" puts someone more at ease than saying "Mumble mumble mumble" and looking around as if you've lost your pocket money. Even if you have lost your pocket money.

3. Start an interaction by asking a question. Secret tip: You can even practice the question beforehand. "So, how long have you been storing your milk cartons?" is a great opener.

DERRING-DO

LEARN THE FIGURE 8 KNOT

Knots are important but they're hard to remember! So I decided to learn ONE. That knot is the Figure 8 knot. Once you learn it, the many variations are simple, and they come in handy for different situations. It's easy to recognize this knot because it looks like the number 8 (if your knot looks like a 7 or a 12, try again!):

Once you've mastered the basic Figure 8 knot, you're ready to try a variation, the Figure 8 on a Loop. The loop is sturdy, perfect for a carabiner. Clip in that popcorn maker and haul it up to your new treehouse! The steps are the same as above, except that you begin with a loop on the rope instead of a single end.

Now you're ready to tie the Figure 8 Follow-through. I use this knot when I want to secure two pieces of rope together. It's easy! Just tie a Figure 8 on one end of a rope (see first illustration), leaving a little bit of tail. Take the end of the other rope and thread it along the first knot, starting at the tail. You're following the first knot from its end to where it started. Try it!

HOW to TIE A FEW key KNOTS

(GO GET SOME ROPE OR STRING)

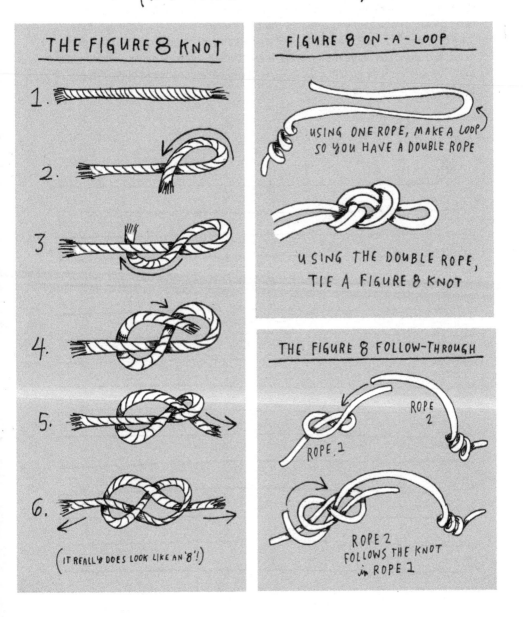

THE FIGURE 8 KNOT

1.

2.

3.

4.

5.

6.

(IT REALLY DOES LOOK LIKE AN '8'!)

FIGURE 8 ON-A-LOOP

USING ONE ROPE, MAKE A LOOP SO YOU HAVE A DOUBLE ROPE

USING THE DOUBLE ROPE, TIE A FIGURE 8 KNOT

THE FIGURE 8 FOLLOW-THROUGH

ROPE 2

ROPE 1

ROPE 2 FOLLOWS THE KNOT in ROPE 1

JOURNAL THIS!

When was the last time you built something with your own hands? Write down what it was, who helped you, and how the process went. Was it ridiculously fun? Was it hard work? If you haven't built anything lately, write down what you want to build, and why. It could be a treehouse, a skateboard ramp, or a milk carton pirate ship! It could even be something you think would be impossible to build, like a spaceship or a skyscraper.

CHAPTER 2

EVEN IF PEOPLE LAUGH
(ESPECIALLY IF PEOPLE LAUGH)

THERE'S A BOOK called the *Guinness Book of World Records*. It's exactly what it sounds like it should be: a document full of world records.

At first that seems sort of boring. Who really cares about the times of track stars, swimmers and race car drivers? Numbers like that are gibberish to most of us. Only the track stars, swimmers and race car drivers are interested. And their moms.

But the *Guinness Book of World Records* isn't boring, because it recognizes feats that are both ordinary and very, very weird. For instance, do you know the record for the longest fingernails? One Mr. Melvin Boothe grew his to a combined length of 32 feet 3.8 inches. That's the equivalent of a three-story building, on your fingers. What about snakes? The longest recorded snake is 25 feet 2 inches. That is five or six of your friends, standing on each other's shoulders. How about the farthest distance that milk has been squirted from an eye? (Yes, people really practice this.) It's 9 feet 2 inches. How about the heaviest weight ever lifted by a human tongue (using a hook through the middle of the tongue. You heard right—HOOK)?

I'm not even going to tell you. It's just too disgusting. (But if you insist, it's 27 pounds 8.96 ounces, which is about the weight of a medium-size dog.)

Perhaps now you can understand why, as a young teenager, I became obsessed with setting a world record. I wanted to take my place in the record books alongside Leslie Tipton (Fastest Time Entering a Suitcase—5.4 seconds!), Sweet Pea (Most Steps Walked Down by a Dog Facing forward and Balancing a Glass of Water on Her Nose—10!) and Charlotte Lee (Largest Collection of Rubber Ducks—5,631!).

But how?

First I needed a compatriot, someone similarly starry-eyed about world records, with physical stamina, grit, and the ability to ignore hoots of disbelieving laughter, should it come to that. My friend Anne fit the bill perfectly. We put our heads together: What feat could we accomplish? We knew we had no real skills, so things like sword swallowing, pogo sticking, and handstands were out. We contemplated trying to set a record in an area no one had thought of before, so that we would be the first. Standing on our heads eating grapes was one idea. Walking on black ice holding a four-layer cake was another. But

SHE SAID...

"Never be limited by other people's imaginations." —**Mae Jemison**, astronaut the world record committee was picky about things like that. They knew there were skill-less people like us scheming to be champions, and they recognized a sham when they saw one. Besides, we wanted to be taken seriously. So we decided to set a world record in an area that was so simple, so basic, so intuitive, that all it would take was our natural determination to shatter the previous record. We had no skills, but we definitely had natural determination.

Crawling.

We had crawled as babies, we reasoned. If we could do it as babies, surely we could do it now. So we hefted open the latest *Guinness Book of World Records* (it was more than 700 pages long) and looked up "crawling."

The record was 12.5 miles.

Now, 12.5 miles is a long way. I had never even walked 12.5 miles. But that day, for some reason, the record seemed as if it would be easy to break. Perhaps it was because we saw the number 1 and the number 2 and not the number 12. 1 and 2 were small numbers! Perhaps we were just naive. Perhaps both. "Crawling it is," said Anne.

We wrote to the *Guinness Book of World Records* and asked what would make a world record official. There had to be witnesses, we were told. There also had to be media coverage.

GIRL HERO!

In 1889, reporter **Nellie Bly** decided to test whether the main character in Jules Verne's popular novel *Around the World in 80 Days* could be bested. Bringing a warm coat, a few changes of underwear, a toiletry bag, and just the dress she was wearing, Bly set off on steamships and trains, sending intermittent reports of her progress back to her newspaper. Meanwhile, a rival newspaper dispatched their own female reporter, hoping to beat Bly. But Bly won, circumnavigating in a world record time of 72 days, 6 hours, 11 minutes, and 14 seconds.

(Now it can take less than 2 hours, though for that you need a spaceship.)

So we called the local newspaper, apprised them of the mighty endeavor, and invited them to cover it. They seemed to think that this was newsworthy, at least after a long pause on the other end of the phone and something that sounded suspiciously like a giggle. Then we asked a few trusted grown-ups, specifically two high school teachers of ours, to witness our feat. They also seemed to think that it was hilarious, but they agreed to help. As dumb as the whole thing sounded, it was hard not to jump on board for a try at a world record.

We didn't tell our friends. Our dream had already provoked disbelief, not to mention snorts and snuffles of barely suppressed laughter. It wasn't just that we were shooting for something so impossible. It was that crawling itself was, well, undignified. So we made our plan in secret. We would crawl around the high school track, which would ensure that the mileage would be accurate. We would do this over spring break, when no one was at school.

You would think that we would have put in some time practicing. But, no. We were relying on our natural will, of which we had a lot, as I have said. The extent of our training amounted to walking to a furniture store to buy large pads of foam. The morning of the world record attempt we put on our good-luck T-shirts and our favorite jeans, tied the foam around our knees with bandanas, and began.

Our first lap, a quarter mile, was a cinch. It took us nine minutes. We crawled together, in rhythm. It probably looked weird but it didn't feel weird. It felt great. We had a dream, and now the dream was coming true.

The sun was out, the day was quiet. This was easy, we thought. Crawling is easy. We began to hope that no one would break our record, once we had set it. Mrs. Starmer sat in a lawn chair with a hat on, marking our progress. Before an hour had even passed, we had crawled a mile. Just 11.6 miles to go.

The next mile was a little slower. But our spirits were high. The photographer from the paper came. He asked us to pose, crawling, under the large scoreboard off to one side. "When we get there," we told him. We couldn't just get up and walk over there. There were rules! The reporter interviewed us. How are you going to go to the bathroom, she asked (everyone wants to know this). We would crawl there, we explained. We just had to maintain the crawling position, and all would be well. This can be done. I am not going to describe it to you, but I assure you, it can be done.

On the third mile, we had exhausted most of what we wanted to talk

GIRL HERO!

 At eleven years old, **Brooke Raboutou** was the youngest person ever to climb a 5.14b rated (translation: super-duper hard) wall. "Only .0001% of climbers can do this," said her coach. Brooke started climbing as soon as she could walk, and both of her parents are elite climbers.

SHE SAID...

"Courage allows the successful woman to fail—and learn powerful lessons from that failure—so that in the end she didn't fail at all." —**Maya Angelou**, poet, author

---

about—who had a crush on who, why that person wasn't so nice, which teacher annoyed us. We crawled in companionable silence. But things were beginning to hurt. Specifically, our knees.

We hadn't bothered to test our equipment. By equipment, I do not mean our brains, which we already understood to be in fine working order (though others might debate that fact). I am speaking of our clothes, and our furniture pads. We had chosen jeans for their durability, but we had failed to consider that denim is a rough and abrasive material. Also, we had tied the protective foam on the outside of our pants, not the inside. Now the rubbing denim was chewing up our skin. Our kneecaps and the backs of our knees where the ties were knotted were badly chafed. Every movement brought worsening pain.

But we forged on. More accurately, we crawled on. And then, at mile 3.8, something else happened that we hadn't expected.

The varsity lacrosse team ran by. Specifically, the boys' varsity lacrosse team.

We had planned everything very carefully. But we had forgotten one thing: the boys' teams arrive back from spring break early, in order to practice.

To say that we were embarrassed does not come close to describing the mortification we felt. We were crawling! On our hands and knees! In front of all the jocks in the school! We were humiliated. But the lacrosse coach had instructed his team that they were not to say a word or even look our way. We were trying to break a world record, he told them, and we were not to be disturbed.

And so they jogged by quietly. When they were gone, we both felt like crying. If you are ever going to attempt a world record, be sure that the boys' lacrosse team is not practicing nearby.

We had been laughed at by adults. Our knees were open sores. Now we were no doubt being laughed at by the boys. Could it get any worse? Yes, it could.

Anne began to get stomach pains. At mile 5.5 she dropped out. Should I continue? I decided that I should. Surely now it couldn't get any worse, I thought.

It began to rain.

Rain is not a big deal in itself. We had raincoats at the ready for just such an eventuality. But as my jeans soaked through and clung to my legs, more chafing occurred. Thousands of tiny piranha teeth seemed to be tearing at my knees.

By now I wanted badly to quit. It was only mile 6 but I had forgotten why I was here. Suddenly the world record seemed stupid. Who was this person who had wanted to crawl more than 12 miles? Clearly there was something very, very wrong with her. My head was hazy with pain and fatigue.

I also couldn't remember why I had decided this was so important. But I had once been clear that it was important. I decided to ignore the doubts I was feeling. I would not let myself be influenced by fatigue and discomfort. I was going to keep crawling.

And so I put my head down and continued to crawl. I ignored the pain. I ignored the rain. And when it got dark, I ignored that, too. But at mile 8 I was shivering, approaching hypothermia. The adult timekeeper, a kind man named Mr. Murphy, said, "I'm not allowing you to go any farther." I may have mumbled something in weak protest but inside there was a part of me—the

SHE SAID...

"What's wrong with this picture?" —**Barbara Hillary**, seventy-five-year-old retired nurse, upon hearing that no African American woman had been to the North Pole. She hired a personal trainer to get in shape, learned to ski, and went.

GIRL HERO!

Quincy Symonds is an Australian skater and surfer nicknamed the Flying Squirrel. She started surfing at four, then picked up skateboarding. At six, she was considered one of the best skaters and surfers of that age in the world.

part of me that was cold, tired, confused, and hurting—that was glad. The other part of me—the part that was warm, alert, certain, focused, and healthy, which was a very small part of me at that moment—was sad. At 8.5 miles, my quest for the world record had ended in failure.

Or was it a failure? Anne and I had failed but we had also dreamed big, which is much better than dreaming small and succeeding. People had laughed and smirked, but we hadn't let that stop us. I had lost sight of my goal at mile six, in a haze of pain and fatigue, but I had had the sense to know that this was a trick of the mind, and I had forged on. Mostly, this had been an adventure.

Now, when I hear of a record being set, I think of those determined girls on the high school track, with their oversize foam padding, oversize grins, and oversize dream. Setting a world record is magnificent. But you know what? Failing to set one is pretty impressive too.

DERRING-DO
THE SELF CONFIDENCE STANCE

There is a reason that Wonder Woman stands like she does, hands on hips, feet apart. It's what scientist Amy Cuddy calls a "high-power pose." It triggers self confidence! High-power poses release chemicals in your body that actually tell your brain that you're feeling pretty great about yourself. "Low-power" poses, such as a hunched back and crossed arms, release chemicals that make you feel pretty lousy and insecure.

Try this: Stand like Wonder Woman for two minutes! You can do this before a world record attempt, before a math test, or before a serious talk with someone who has been mean to you. You can do this in secret, or you can do it with all your friends. Let the confidence chemicals flow!

WONDER WOMAN POSE

EYES STRAIGHT AHEAD

SLIGHT SMILE

WEIGHT CENTERED

HANDS ON HIPS

FEET APART

DERRING-DO
RECOGNIZING ANIMAL TRACKS!

I spent a lot of time staring at the ground during my crawling world record attempt. I saw lots of sneaker prints and, of course, many knee prints. But could I recognize animal prints?

Try this: Take a walk in the woods along an animal trail. Or check out a sandy patch at your local park. If you see four pads with claws, you are looking at the paw of a dog, or an animal from the dog family. If you see four pads with no claws, you are looking at the paw of a cat, or an animal from the cat family. NOTE: If any of those pads are huge, and you are not a lion tamer or a member of a wolf pack, run away very quickly!

Tip: When inspecting tracks, keep them between you and the sun for best lighting. If it is nighttime, don't shine the flashlight beam directly on the ground in front of you, but aim it parallel to the ground; this way you won't wash out the prints in the glare.

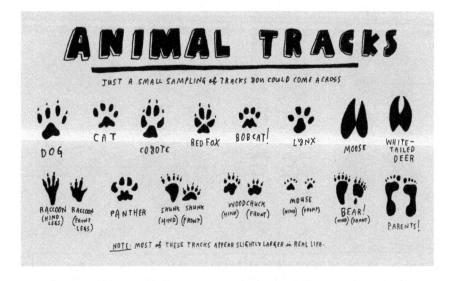

ANIMAL TRACKS

JUST A SMALL SAMPLING of TRACKS you COULD COME ACROSS

DOG   CAT   COYOTE   RED FOX   BOBCAT!   LYNX   MOOSE   WHITE-TAILED DEER

RACCOON (HIND LEGS)   RACCOON (FRONT LEGS)   PANTHER   SKUNK (HIND)   SKUNK (FRONT)   WOODCHUCK (HIND)   (FRONT)   MOUSE (HIND)   (FRONT)   BEAR! (HIND)   (FRONT)   PARENTS!

NOTE: MOST of THESE TRACKS APPEAR SLIGHTLY LARGER in REAL LIFE.

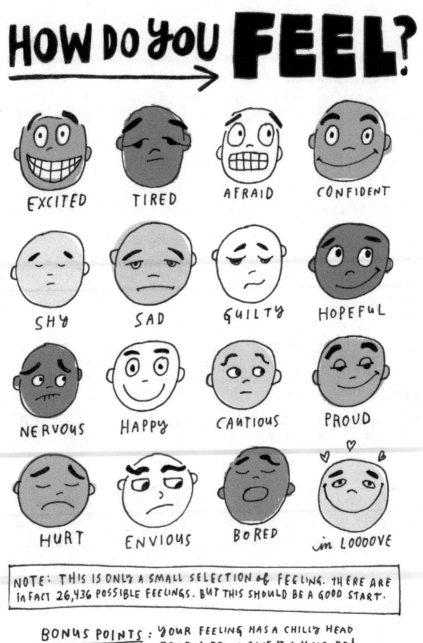

DERRING-DO
KEEP AN ADVENTURE JOURNAL!

Everyone loves to read about adventure (I hope so. This is an adventure book). Why not begin to write down yours? Remember, you don't have to scale a high mountain. An adventure can be as simple as riding your bike, with your friend, on a new road. Did you raise your hand in class for the very first time this year despite the fact it scared the bejeezus out of you? That's adventurous too!

Try this: Keep a journal of your adventures. Write down all the details of the event, but remember to include how you felt, too. Confident? Nervous? Proud? Sometimes it's difficult to describe emotions, so feel free to use the How Do You Feel chart on the opposite page. Remember, you don't have to show this journal to anyone. Or you can bind it between two covers and make a book that you hand out to friends and family. It's up to you!

JOURNAL THIS!

Start your adventure journal by writing about your most recent adventure. What did you do? Who were you with? What challenges were there? How did you overcome them? Most important, how did you feel during the adventure? If you'd like, use the How Do You Feel chart on page 26! Pick the words that most accurately describe your emotions, or just circle the faces that apply if that's more fun. Go!

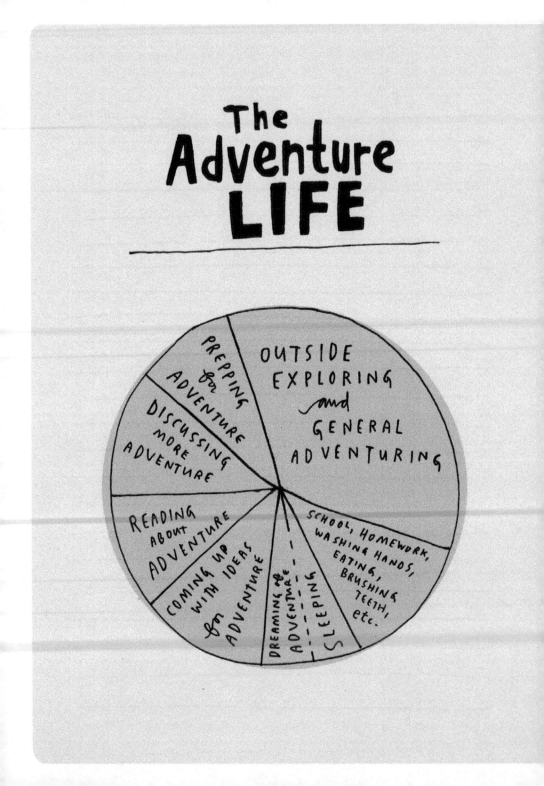

The UN-Adventure LIFE

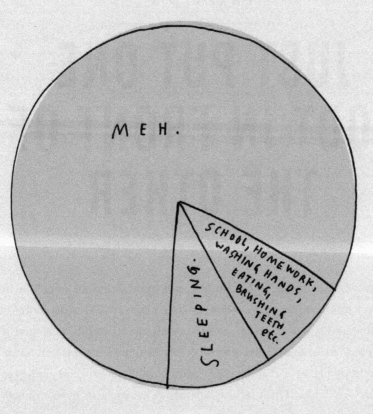

VERY, VERY TALL

CHAPTER 3

JUST PUT ONE FOOT IN FRONT OF THE OTHER

SOME THINGS ARE meant to be climbed, and some things are not. Take, for example, a mountain. It's not a mountain unless some wild-haired, sunburnt-nosed, strange-sunglass-wearing, semi-toeless alpinist claims she must give it a shot. Or how about an oak tree—one with low-hanging arms that curl upward and a perfectly placed burl at the base. "Must climb!" squeal third graders and squirrels. Or a ladder. That's self-explanatory. A ladder exists to be climbed.

But a bridge?

This is why, when my friend Trina announced that she wanted to climb a bridge, a very famous bridge, one called the Golden Gate Bridge, I should have said, "Huh?" And when she asked if I wanted to join, along with a few other friends, I should have said, "Join?"

Instead I said, "Yes."

The plan for our team of five—all female, it turned out—was to walk along a swooping suspension cable until we reached the top. As I mentioned, this was a famous bridge; I bring that up not to boast, but to point out that famous bridges are rarely small. So these particular swooping suspension cables on this particular famous bridge not only swooped with the exaggerated grandeur due famous things, but they went up really, really high—746 feet, to be exact, the equivalent of a 76-story skyscraper. Which sounded awesome. And very, very scary. So we weighed the facts, like good adventurers should: scary vs awesome.

Awesome won.

On the appointed night we arrived at the base of the bridge. We stared, taking in the joints and ribs above us. We didn't say anything to each other but we knew what we were thinking. Wow!, Jeez!, Heck!, Yikes! was what we were thinking, and it all translated to mean only one thing: It's a long, long, long way to the top.

Wait! Before I continue, I must add that climbing the Golden Gate Bridge is not just terrifying. It's illegal. I'm not in any way suggesting that you, too, should lead a life of bridge-climbing crime. I even considered not including this story for fear that you would immediately begin to rob banks, trespass

SHE SAID...

"When I'm on a really high climb I look down. I'm not scared. It's just so cool to think how small I am compared to the rock, and how high I am."

—Brooke Raboutou, eleven years old, world-class rock climber

onto private property, run while at the pool, make faces at emotional support dogs, and even fail to give up your seat up on the bus to an elderly man. But I have faith in you, Gutsy Girl. You will read this story the way it should be read—as a lesson in managing fear and not as a blueprint for a life of crime. You will finish these pages realizing that this is one of the more stupid things I've done and that you—much smarter—will always mind the signs that read Stop, Do Not Enter, and Don't Even Think About It.

Okay. Back to our story.

"Ready?" Trina whispered, as we pulled caps onto our heads, tied our shoe-laces in double knots (no one wanted to trip), and did some quick about-to-climb-a-very-long-way-to-the-top yoga stretches. Did I mention that walking up the suspension cable of the Golden Gate Bridge is not allowed? (Yes I did, but it bears mentioning again, with a sigh and a waggle of the finger.) So this was midnight, on a Tuesday, and we wore all black and spoke in low voices. One by one we gave the thumbs up. One by one we clambered up and over the chicken-wire fence. This fence was supposed to be a deterrent to such ventures, but chicken wire is only a deterrent to chickens, and chickens we were not, in any sense of the word.

The city glittered. The wind was quiet. Cars sped by below us, unaware. There were guide wires that acted as banisters for our hands and a cable with enough room to put one foot in front of the other quite safely, if carefully. This

---

GIRL HERO!

 Marie Antoine began climbing trees for fun when she was four. Now she climbs for a living and is one of just a few botanists who work in the canopies of the tallest living things in the world—the redwood tree. You can often find her eating lunch or sleeping in a hammock 325 feet in the air.

wasn't going to be a climb. This was going to be a walk. I thought to myself, I know how to walk! No problem!

But very quickly the ground dropped away. The lights of the city tilted and spread, and the wind picked up. I kept my eyes on my feet to make sure each step landed where it should, and this was fine, but if I was going to look at my feet I was also going to have to see how far away Earth was becoming. It was becoming very far away indeed.

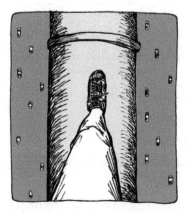

The speeding cars were now speeding Matchbox toys. What had been land on one side of us disappeared, replaced by ocean. Or at least I assumed it was ocean. I couldn't see anything beyond a black abyss. Every so often this abyss flashed a line of white, and with a whisper the surf crashed against the cliffs.

It wasn't very long before I decided that I was not superhuman when it came to heights. I was actually quite average, with the normal reflexes of any creature who had an intact brain and solid survival instincts. Those reflexes included watery legs, sweat, and a voice in my head that suddenly shouted, *There's hundreds of feet of NOTHINGNESS below you!!!*

I took a deep breath, trying to calm down. This is just a walk, I reminded myself.

"Sure, a walk above JUST AIR," the voice interrupted.

"Okay, whoa. You be quiet," I said. I recognized the voice, with the same sinking feeling one gets when an uninvited guest walks into a birthday party. Not just any uninvited guest. One nobody likes very much, who hogs the birthday cake and cheats at the games. This uninvited guest was Fear, and right now she was really not welcome. So I tried to make my own voice stern.

SHE SAID...

"Stand[ing] on a shaky one-inch line over an abyss, every iota of my body was telling me not to be there! I was challenging thousands of years of evolution [that told me] to stay away from the cliff edge." —**Faith Dickey**, professional tightrope walker (also known as a slackliner), on her first attempt to walk across a rope hundreds of feet in the air. She has since walked across many abysses, including four thousand feet above the valley floor in the Swiss Alps.

But it was too late. I glanced around me, and the cable did suddenly look quite frail. The wire handrails of hardened steel now felt like toothpicks. It was a long way down.

"Just piping up to keep you safe!" Fear called out.

"Really? Because you're just getting in the way."

Fear sounded offended. "I like to think I'm the voice of reason."

"Reason says this is just a walk. Look." I nod to the cable. "It's just one foot in front of the other. I've done that a trillion times."

"Really?" Here Fear craned her neck as if measuring how far the fall would be. "You've done this on the thirty-fifth floor of a skyscraper? Which is where you are at this moment. Heading to the seventieth? Just checking."

Maybe it would be easier to go down right now.

"Now you're thinking," Fear said. "Get out while the getting out is good. What if there's an earthquake? Or a bridge collapse? Or a brief but catastrophic downpour?"

The cars were ants now. The surf was just a distant hiss. I felt tiny against the panorama of city lights, water, steel, and night air around me. The top of the bridge loomed, and its huge shadow was thrown across the sky like a monster. Behind me everyone was moving slowly and steadily. No one was whimpering or weeping. No one was frozen with fear. Clearly their heebie-jeebies were under control. Why was I such a wimp?

More importantly, I had many emotions right now, so why did Fear get center stage?

And so I did what I usually do when I feel afraid. I called all my feelings to attention, like a drill sergeant at boot camp. I marched Exhilaration at Doing Something So Daring out front. I placed Wonder at the View right behind. I told So Fun to Have an Adventure to get in line, too. Finally, I allowed Fear to tag along.

"You're there, but I'm not concentrating on you!" I told Fear.

This time it was Fear who whined. "Come on! Look how far down it is!"

I ignored her. My next steps were taken with Exhilaration. I marveled at the vista spread out below me with Wonder. Look, Coit Tower! See, Alcatraz Island! And to our right was the squat (and much easier to climb, I was betting) Bay Bridge. I still had a death grip on the cable and sweat trickling down my back, but Fun wasn't letting Fear push her from her place in line. The butterflies were there, too. But I concentrated on all the other feelings instead.

Then Beth called out, "Red lights!"

From the ground we had seen two strange red lights about halfway up the cable. We'd feared that they were security cameras. We'd contemplated all the things action heroes do when confronted with security cameras.

1. They disconnect them using technical wizardry.

GIRL HERO!

Ashima Shiraishi was thirteen years old when she climbed a bouldering route called Golden Shadow, in South Africa. It's graded V14 on the bouldering scale (translation: So Hard Only the Best are Doing It) in a rating system that tops out at V16. "Bouldering" describes a climb that is no higher than twenty-five feet from the ground. The climber does not wear a harness, but can be protected by a pad at the base of the rock.

---

2. They shoot them out of commission with a weapon.

3. They use grappling hooks to rappel around them.

We wished we were action heroes, but we were not. We decided to do what mere mortals do: We hid our faces and waddled by as quickly as possible. Soon enough we would know if we had been seen.

The pitch steepened. I had to walk on my toes. The wire left grooves on my palms. We were five tiny dots on a huge metal structure high in the air. But my fear was well in check. She loped in the back of the line, while the emotions in front cheered me on. The top was close. And then it was there.

I lay down on the wide crosspiece like a sailor dropping to her knees on land after a storm. One by one my intrepid teammates climbed from the cable to the platform and lay down next to me. We had done it! Amazing. Then I heard:

"I'm going up there." It was Trina.

I lifted my head. Up where? Weren't we at the top?

Turns out, NO.

On either side of us the towers reared upward twenty more feet. At the crest of each was a small flat spot bounded by low guardrails. In the middle stood a red light, probably meant to warn low-flying aircraft. As we watched, Trina bounded over to the ladder and began to climb. At the top, she pulled herself up. For a moment I thought that was that. She would stay crouched there, and come down. But slowly she began to rise, slowly, slowly. Finally she was fully standing. She raised her arms over her head, a black silhouette against the night sky, higher than anything for miles around. Then she let out a huge shout. She was at the tippy-tippy-top of the bridge, and grinning from ear to ear.

SHE SAID...

"Adventures don't come calling like unexpected cousins calling from out of town. You have to go looking for them."—**Unknown**

GIRL HEROES!

In the mid-1990s a group of women on the Yankton Sioux/Ihanktonwan Oyate Reservation in South Dakota realized that the young girls of their tribe needed traditional knowledge and rituals in order to prepare for the complications of life ahead. They named themselves the **Brave Heart Society**, and reinstated a four-day event called the Isnati Awica Dowanpi coming-of-age ceremony. It includes gathering herbs and flowers for medicines, raising a tepee and sleeping in it as a group for four days, and listening to older girls and women pass on advice and stories.

If Trina can do it, can't I? I got slowly to my feet. My heart, which had slowed, began to pump hard again. My breathing, which had also slowed, quickened. I reached the ladder, waited for Trina to descend, then began to climb. Come on, Fun! Step up, Exhilaration! Where are you, Wonder?

When the ladder ended, I slithered onto the flat area. I lay there, taking in the fact that there was only air around me, and the sky seemed so close. Then, inch by inch, I slid one foot under me, then the other, until I was crouching on the tiny pad. I closed my eyes, and . . . couldn't stand up. *Stand up!* I yelled at myself. *Stand up!* But I was frozen. This was my limit. "I can't do it," I groaned. I stayed there, breathing. It wasn't elegant, and I wasn't on my feet, but I was at the tippy-tippy-top, and my friends cheered.

We took photos of ourselves looking windblown and ecstatic, then glanced at our watches and agreed it was time to go. For a moment I wondered, but what about the red-lighted security camera? Hadn't we been seen? I eyed the elevator doors (yes, there is an elevator, for smart people) willing them to open and spill out security guards who would look at us sternly, sigh, and escort us back down the easy way. But the elevator doors didn't open. The red lights weren't security cameras, they were just red lights, probably for very, very low-flying planes. There would be no ride with security guards in the safety of an elevator. Besides, that wouldn't be fun. I clambered back onto the cable, faced the tiny cars and the thumb-size street lamps, set my feet firmly, gripped the guide wires tightly, and began to walk.

DERRING-DO
THE STALKING STEP

There are many ways to walk, depending on where you are. On the bridge I progressed with tiny steps, one in front of the other. But what if you come upon an animal in the wild and want to get a closer look? Survivalist Tom Brown Jr. recommends what he calls the Stalking Step. (NOTE: This walking method is also useful if you're raiding the kitchen in the middle of the night.)

Try this: Brown says the Stalking Step must be smooth, continuous, and evenly paced. It must also be very, very slow—almost a minute will elapse between the time the foot leaves the ground and touches again! Begin in a crouched position, with your arms close to your body, and your foot proceeding in a slow, high arc off the ground. The foot lands (a minute later) on the outside ball area, rolling inward until the ball is on the ground. Only then does the heel drop slowly down, shifting weight onto it. If the animal (or your parent) looks your way, STOP mid-stride and remain that way until the animal/parent relaxes again.

DERRING-DO
FIND THE NORTH STAR!

If you're out at night, and not busy climbing a bridge, take a look above you. For thousands of years our ancestors used the North Star to navigate, and you can, too.

Try this: To find the North Star, first find the Big Dipper. (If you live in a city, that's fine. It can still be easy to spot.) This constellation looks like a large water scooper (or "dipper") in the sky. (It may be facing up, down, or sideways. It changes throughout the night and the seasons!) Find the part of the water scooper that would contain the water (this is made up of four stars in a rectangle). Then imagine holding the handle (three bright stars that extend crookedly from the rectangle) and pouring water out of the scooper. The side that the water pours from is made up of two stars. We call these the "pointer stars" because when you follow the line of those two stars (in the direction the water would flow) you arrive at the North Star. It's not very bright, but it's easy to spot, because it's the brightest star in the vicinity. You are now facing north! NOTE: If you live in the Southern Hemisphere, you won't see the North Star. But your sky has the beautiful Southern Cross constellation!

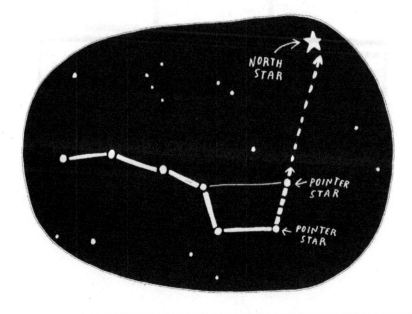

NORTH STAR

← POINTER STAR

← POINTER STAR

DERRING-DO
BRAIN GAME

You'd like to make the soccer team, but your kick lacks power or accuracy. Don't despair. You can improve a lot! Why? Because your brain is built to adapt. It wants to learn to get better, and it physically changes in order to do this, beefing up neural pathways, and configuring more efficient routes from its command center to all the muscles in your foot. The best way to encourage physical change that translates into learning? Repetition! Kick that ball over and over and over and over, and your brain will perfect this new skill. Welcome to the soccer team!

Try This: Pick a skill you'd like to improve. Knot tying? Ball throwing? Do it fifteen times every day for the next week.

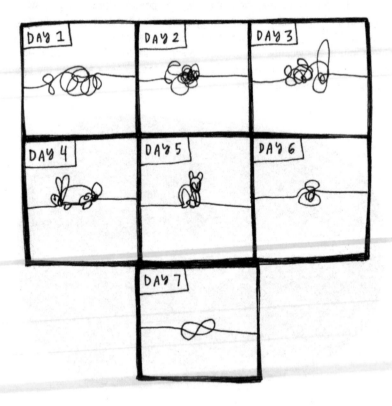

JOURNAL THIS!

Knowing your feelings is the first step to dealing with any kind of adverse situations. When I climbed the bridge I recognized my fear, but I recognized my exhilaration too. What are you feeling right now? Using the emotion chart on page 26, identify the faces that best describe those feelings. Draw those below.

Now write down what you think might be the reason for each emotion you've illustrated.

STEP 1: TURN BOOK

SHOULD YOU JUMP OFF THAT CLIFF?

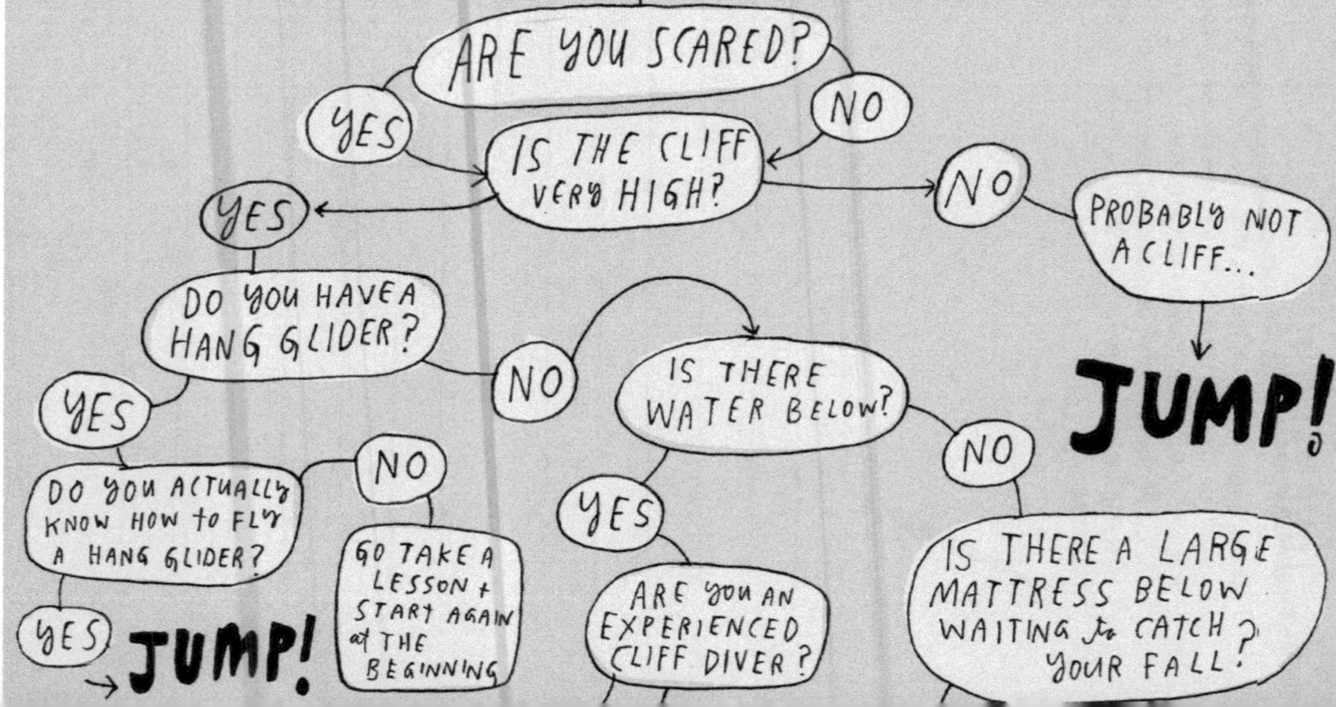

STEP 2: USE FLOWCHART

CHAPTER 4

AIM HIGH! BUT, SOMETIMES, NOT TOO HIGH

I'VE ALWAYS WANTED to fly like a bird. But how? I was a human with two legs, two arms, and opposable thumbs. What I needed was wings.

When I was eighteen, I signed up for flying lessons. I settled behind the yoke of a rickety Cessna 150, and soon enough I was a private pilot. I enjoyed speeding down the runway, lurching into the air, and chugging over the patch-

GIRL HERO!

Mae Jemison went to Stanford University at sixteen, and after a career as a physician in countries such as Kenya, Sierra Leone, and Liberia, she applied to the NASA space program to be an astronaut. In 1992 she became the first African American woman in space.

Since then she has been a professor at Cornell University, and the founder of multiple tech companies.

work of towns and fields. But something was missing. Or more accurately, too much was not missing. Where was the wind in my feathers (or in my case, feathered hair, all the rage at the time)? Where was the feeling of being suspended above the earth, nothing below but my feet and air? In the Cessna I was encased in aluminum and glass. This was not flying like a bird. This was flying like a can of soup.

But then paragliding came along. To most people (such as insurance agents and mothers), a paraglider looks like a bedsheet with strings trailing off the sides. That's pretty accurate, except a paraglider is a bedsheet in the shape of a wing, and wing shapes do one thing very well. They fly.

So just attach those strings to a harness, sit in the harness, grab the toggles with each opposable thumb (and some fingers), and start running. Run right off of a cliff and, voilà, you're flying like a bird!*

I loved paragliding. I soared above beaches, riding the breezes that hit the cliffs and pushed upward, providing what we humans in the flying world called "lift" and what our feathered friends just called "life." For hours I'd float, watching the hawks and seagulls nearby, pretending to be one of them.

---

* I have simplified the process for the purposes of what we writers call narrative flow, or Don't Bore Your Reader. Some steps I haven't mentioned: run into bushes, run into dips in the hill, run until you are so tired you can't run anymore, run hoping your bedsheet/wing inflates above you, run until your bedsheet/wing does inflate above you, run until inflating your bedsheet/wing is a piece of cake, and THEN run off of the cliff. And fly like a bird.

GIRL HERO!

Bessie "Queen Bess" Coleman (January 26, 1892–April 30, 1926) was a famous barnstorming pilot and parachutist. At the age of twenty-three she traveled to France to train for her pilot's license, after American flight schools refused her because she was female and black. Once she returned home, crowds were awed by her daring stunts and flying skill and she became wildly popular at air shows. Astronaut Mae Jemison first went into space with a picture of Queen Bess among her possessions.

Then one day my flying friends Lars and Mike suggested that we expand our paragliding horizons and travel to the far-off country of Brazil. There we would find the world's best thermal flying.

I was a fine paraglider, with a fine amount of experience. But I knew very little about thermal flying. When I say Very Little what I really mean is Pretty Much Nothing, but Very Little is what I told concerned friends and family. You can see that "very little" isn't that comforting, but it did sound better when I added, "And I'm going with my friend Lars and he knows very much about thermal flying." Which was true. Once on the mountain in Brazil, Lars explained the basics to me. Then he said, "It'll be no problem. It's really easy."

Now, Lars was an extraordinary person. He was a world-class kayaker, a world-class climber. He was the kind of guy who had been caught in inhumane weather conditions and survived, who knew how to build an igloo, start a fire with a shoelace, and perform a precordial thump. When Lars said it was easy, he meant it was easy FOR HIM. Unfortunately, I was just an ordinary person, and things were never that easy for me. But Lars was also the kind of guy everybody wanted to impress, me included, and so I decided not to point this out. Nor did I request any additional tips after his very brief instruction on thermal flying. I just casually nodded in agreement—of course it's easy—and in no time the three of us were zipping up our flight suits, pulling our paragliders from their backpacks, laying them on the ground, and climbing into our harnesses. Meanwhile this was my inner monologue: I've spent my paragliding days doing a type of flying called Ridge Soaring. Thermal flying is different. But maybe finding lift is finding lift. So what's the big deal?

I should pause to point out that whenever you say to yourself So What's the Big Deal, it usually means there is a Big Deal. You should immediately rephrase to say What a Big Deal! in order to be fully prepared for the journey ahead.

But I did not rephrase. Instead I clipped my harness to the lines. Mike straightened the edges of my wing—not because they needed it but because he wanted to communicate that he had my back, though there was little either he or Lars could do once I took to the air. For this reason flying a paraglider has at once been the most exhilarating and the most lonely thing I have ever done.

I launched.

Lars and Mike and the mountain receded behind me. Two thousand feet below my flying boots, the land stretched out in browns and greens. It was quiet except for the whisper of air through the wing above me, and the congenial beeping of the variometer on my shoulder.

A variometer is a device pilots depend on in thermal flying. It measures a gain or loss in altitude by emitting beeps that rise in pitch as the paraglider ascends in the sky, and that descend in pitch as it drops to the ground. We humans need this audible warning because it's hard to gauge our place in the sky with the variometer we use on earth—our eyes, ears, and stomach. Right now the lowering baritone told me that I was losing altitude. I was going to have to do something about that, fast.

SHE SAID...

"Woman can if she will." —**Augusta Van Buren**, who rode a motorcycle from New York to Mexico in 1916 with her sister, Adeline

VARIOMETER

I quickly enumerated the very brief points Lars had made about thermal flying in his very brief lesson.

1. Hot air rises.

2. Paragliders can ride this hot air, called a thermal, upward.

3. A thermal is column-shaped, so you have to circle your paraglider to stay in it, like the birds do.

4. Circling birds are good. They show you exactly where a thermal is, because otherwise a thermal is invisible.

5. Cumulus clouds (those fluffy white clouds on a sunny day) are good. This is where the hot air of a thermal has cooled and stopped, forming a cloud. Where there is a cumulus cloud, there is a thermal!

It occurred to me then: Finally, I was really going to be flying like a bird.

I spotted a fluffy cumulous cloud to my right and I headed that way. Up to this point flight using invisible columns of rising air seemed impossible. But lo and behold my variometer's beep started to rise: ooAAEEEE!!!, it sang in my ear. I was climbing! In a thermal!

Within seconds I was dropping again: EEeaaaooooooooo went the variometer. I'd forgotten to circle, so I'd passed right through it. Still, this was good.

GIRL HERO!

Photojournalist **Alison Wright** travels to the steppes of Mongolia, the steeps of Nepal, islands off Africa, and Tibetan temples for her work. She has documented the aftermath of tsunamis and earthquakes, befriended the Dalai Lama, climbed Kilamanjaro, and been gifted a warthog tusk by a Masai woman. Her high school English teacher encouraged her interest in photography, explaining that photojournalism could become a viable career. "I was fifteen or sixteen when I discovered what I wanted to do with my life, and I've never wavered."

SHE SAID...

"It feels freaking amazing!" —**Shannon Fitzgerald D'Alessio**, on being part of a successful skydiving world record attempt

---

This was easy.[*]

With this false confidence I was already forming the story I was going to tell Lars and Mike, how I had hopped from thermal to thermal until the daylight ran out. In the distance I could see birds circling. Birds Circling! That was Point Number 4 in Lars' Very Brief Lesson on Thermal Flying. I headed that way.

Four happy raptors spun below me like burly Olympic skaters on an invisible rink. They didn't break away from the thermal when they saw me, didn't even seem to mind that I was on their turf. Perhaps they recognized me for what I was: a clumsy, wingless human flying a bedsheet, who had biffed the last thermal and probably didn't stand a chance catching this one. But abruptly I was bounced in my harness; one wingtip had found rising air. My variometer squealed happily. I made a sharp turn and suddenly I was circling. I was grinning, circling, grinning: ooeeeeEEEEEEEEEEEEEEEEE shrieked the variometer happily as up, Up, UP I went. Quickly I left the birds behind, and the checkerboard ground shrank away.

Hot air cools as it rises, and Lars had been very clear that at the bottom of the cloud I would stop. Wasn't that what he'd said? I thought that was what he'd said. But now the air started to mist. I wasn't stopping, or even slowing. In fact, I was ascending faster. My variometer had gone from enthusiasm to what sounded like mild panic, so I leveled my wing. This didn't appease the variometer at all. I was still rising. Within a moment the mist turned to fog.

My variometer was now unmistakably screaming at me. EEEEEEEEEEEE,

---

[*] Saying This Was Easy so early in the game is always a bad sign.

SHE SAID...

"Daring makes a difference." —**Mae Jemison**, astronaut

it cried. Meanwhile, my stomach dropped (EEeeeeoooooooooooooooo).

I realized what was happening, just as the cloud completely enveloped me.

It was called Cloud Suck. It happened when you thought you were flying below a cumulus cloud, but you were really below a building cumulonimbus. The difference between those two clouds doesn't sound like a big deal. Cumulus means "heap" in Latin. But in Latin the word "nimbus" means "dark cloud." In other words a cumulus cloud was just a heap of clouds, but a cumulonimbus cloud was one of those black, towering, anvil-shaped monsters that you associate with an incoming storm.

I was in a thundercloud.

TOWERING CUMULONIMBUS

I'd heard all the stories. Visibility goes from white to black. You're rained on, hailed on, and lightning flashes on all sides. At some point you lose consciousness. Your wing begins to freeze. You are finally spat out and you're probably dead. If you're not, your wing has been ripped to shreds and you soon will be. One paraglider pilot, a European champion, had been cloud-sucked to thirty-two thousand feet—that's where jetliners fly. This was recorded on her variometer, which froze there. She survived only because she gained consciousness on her descent, her paraglider miraculously intact, and guided herself to the ground.

I had only seconds before the white-out transformed into the storm part of the cloud. It was not a lot of time to think. This was unfortunate, because I'm not that quick a thinker to begin with. So I simply reacted. I performed a basic maneuver that I had done many times before, called Big Ears. I folded the wing tips inward so that the surface area of the paraglider decreased, making the wing smaller. This had always worked well on California spring days when I wanted to descend out of rough air. But this wasn't just rough air. This was cloud suck. So I pulled BIG Big Ears, folding much more than just the wing tips, and transformed my paraglider into something closer to an umbrella.

This did nothing at all! My variometer kept screaming. EEEEEEEE EEEEEEEEEEEEE. I kept climbing. The white began to darken.

I had two other tricks up my sleeve and I only had a few seconds to pick one and hope it worked. The first was called the spiral dive. This entailed great g-forces as you whiplashed in circles to the ground. The second choice was to stall. This meant collapsing the wing so that it would no longer be wing-shaped. It would be Fluttering-Ball-of-Bedsheet-shaped. And I would no longer be flying; I would be dropping. Dropping like a stone, something I had never wished for in my life but which sounded pretty good right about then.

Stalling the wing would be the most effective. I had practiced this maneuver before, but I had never liked it. It was an extreme maneuver and it had

SHE SAID...

"So, let's see, well . . . except for Hurricane Luci, who just came blasting over the top of New Zealand, not too many exciting things happened." —**Laura Dekker**, fifteen-year-old solo sailor, talking about a typical day on board her boat, Guppy

one small problem. Sometimes the chute didn't reopen. I could be a stone all the way to the ground. This was not what I wanted. What should I do? The spiral dive or the stall? If the one I picked didn't work, I would not have time to perform the other. I'd be deep into the thundercloud by then.

I decided on the spiral dive, but to make sure it worked I also decided to stay in Big Ears. Weren't two maneuvers put together better than just one?*

Actually, the g-forces from combining two maneuvers could rip the lines from the wing. Part of me was well aware of this. But I was being cloud-sucked. So the other part of me thought, "What the heck!"**

I rocketed out of the bottom of that storm cloud, spinning and dropping like a downed war plane. Luck was with me, and my wing held. Skill was with me, too, as I gently transitioned out of the two maneuvers and leveled off. EEEeeeeeee went my exhaled breath. Ba BOOM, Ba BOOM went my heart. I glided for a while, calming down. I was both ashamed of my mistake, and exhilarated to be alive. Was there a lesson here? I had tried to learn something new, but I had almost killed myself doing it. Still, I hadn't killed myself.

Suddenly it was clear to me: The best outdoor athletes are adventurous, but they aren't reckless! They know their skill level, and their goals. So if you've mastered a single flip off a twenty-foot cliff into water and a double flip on a trampoline, you can probably try that double flip from the cliff. But if you've

* If you have to ask yourself this, the answer is probably no.

** I do not have to tell you that *What the Heck!* is not a good reason to do anything, do I?

only been practicing a belly flop, don't even think about it. Being reckless is not being gutsy, it's being stupid. I was inexperienced enough to get cloud-sucked. But I was experienced enough to un-cloud-suck myself, too.

One thing was for sure, I wasn't going to say a word to anyone about this. Especially not to Lars.

When we regrouped at the landing zone, Lars and Mike wanted to know how my flight had been. They'd lost sight of me, Lars said, after their own launches. "Oh, I'm getting the hang of it," I said, shrugging with feigned nonchalance.

Lars looked happy. "Pretty great, right?!" he cried. Then his eyes widened, and his voice lowered. "Well, I don't want to freak you out." He leaned in closer. "But I saw this dude get cloud sucked. Cumulonimbus! He escaped, though." Lars shook his head. "I don't know who it was but man, that guy was brave, and jeez, was he stupid!"

DERRING-DO
CALM YOURSELF

When we're nervous or stressed, our breathing becomes shallow and fast. Certain breathing techniques help to calm and focus.

Try this: Inhale through your nose into your belly, to a count of four. Hold to a count of four. Exhale through your mouth, pulling in your belly as far as you can, to a count of four. Hold again to a count of four. Repeat three more times.

DERRING-DO
MICROBRAVERY!

"Bravery takes practice," says Rachel Simmons of Girls Leadership. So she encourages microbravery—taking action in situations that may not be terrifying but nevertheless demand courage. Are you scared of that spider on the table? Of course you are! That doesn't mean you can't take four deep breaths, gently urge it onto a piece of paper, and carry it outside to freedom.

Try this: For the next week, perform five acts of microbravery. Write them down. Remember, finding your courage is much like finding your best swing in softball. It takes practice!

DERRING-DO
RECOGNIZE CLOUDS!

When air rises to cooler altitudes, its moisture turns from vapor to liquid, forming a cloud. This process is called condensation. Clouds are categorized by their shape and their altitudes.

Try this: Walk outside and look up. What clouds are in the sky right now?

Cirrus: Found at high altitudes, they look thin and wispy. They indicate calm, fair weather, but if they increase, the weather will be changing! Watch the direction they move, and you'll know where the weather is coming from.

Cumulus: These puffy cotton balls are fair-weather clouds if they are spaced far apart. But if they continue to build, they become the dreaded cumulonimbus, also known as a towering thunderhead. Get out your rain jackets (and steer your paragliders away).

Stratus: Covering the whole sky, this dull, gray sheet of cloud doesn't usually bring rain until it darkens to become nimbostratus; then be prepared for sustained rain or snow.

Dreamlandus: The expression "having your head in the clouds" means "you're daydreaming/not paying attention." I mention this cloud (which I just made up) because my head was clearly in a dreamlandus when I got myself into a cumulonimbus.

JOURNAL THIS!

List four people who you admire. Write down the qualities in them that are so inspiring (Humor? Good cooking skills? Mean fastball? Kindness? Pizzazz?) Think how you can incorporate those qualities into your own life. Look at this list when you need guidance. Look at this list when you want inspiration. Look at this list just for fun! After all, who doesn't need a shot of Amazing now and then?

ADVENTURE KIT
☑CHECKLIST☑

☐ **MIRROR** for SIGNALING. (SIGNALING IS DIFFICULT and TAKES PRACTICE. DO NOT DIRECT SUNLIGHT into ANYONE'S EYES. EVEN IF YOU DON'T LIKE THEM.)

☐ **WHISTLE** BECAUSE NO MATTER WHAT YOUR TEACHER TELLS YOU YOUR YELLING IS JUST NOT LOUD ENOUGH.

☐ **CLEAR PLASTIC GARBAGE BAGS** (5 TOTAL
   1 for AN EMERGENCY PONCHO.
   1 to COLLECT WATER (SEE CHAPTER 7 DERRING-DOs.)
   3 to RIG A TARP SHELTER. CUT THE BAGS SO THEY MAKE LARGE SQUARES. DUCT TAPE THEM TOGETHER.

☐ **PARACHUTE CORD** WHICH IS MADE UP OF LOTS OF SMALLER PIECES OF CORD. THIS WAY YOU CARRY SO MUCH MORE ROPE, USEFUL for RIGGING UP TARPS, MAKING SPLINTS, etc.

☐ **KNIFE** BECAUSE YOU ALWAYS NEED A KNIFE.

☐ **LIGHTER** BUT ONLY IF YOU'RE OLD ENOUGH.

☐ **CLEAR, CALM MINDSET**, WHICH MAY NOT BE VISIBLE INSIDE YOUR ADVENTURE KIT. BUT IT'S THERE READY to BE PULLED OUT WHEN NEEDED.

☐ **COTTON BALLS DOUSED IN VASELINE, STORED IN A FILM CANISTER.** THESE ARE <u>VERY FLAMMABLE</u> and CAN BE USED to START A FIRE, but ONLY IF YOU'RE OLD ENOUGH.

☐ **COMPASS** BECAUSE EVEN IF YOU'RE LOST, YOU CAN STILL BECOME UN-LOST.

☐ **IODINE TABLETS** to PURIFY WATER BECAUSE YOU ALWAYS NEED CLEAN WATER to DRINK.

☐ **FLASHLIGHT** of COURSE.

☐ **DUCT TAPE** (TAKE IT OFF THE ROLL by WRAPPING A VERY LONG PIECE AROUND YOUR FLASHLIGHT. MUCH LIGHTER!) THIS CAN BE USED to SPLINT INJURIES, REPAIR TEARS in TENTS and CLOTHES, EVEN TIE YOUR HAIR UP, THOUGH ONLY DO THAT IF YOU REALLY, REALLY NEED A HAIR TIE.

☐ **ZIPLOCK BAG** (LARGE) in WHICH to PUT ALL THESE ITEMS.

STRAP to BACK, WHEELCHAIR, ADVENTURE BUDDY (ie. DOG)

POCKET for PENS, GLASSES, GOGGLES, EMERGENCY CANDY

CHAPTER 5

WHAT GOES UP, MIGHT COME DOWN

OF THE MANY mountains in Alaska, there is one more spectacular than the rest. The Alaska State tourism bureau praises this mountain for its beauty (unparalleled) and its height (tallest in North America), but what this mountain is really known for, at least among mountain climbers, is its weather. People die in its terrible blizzards. They're blown off the mountain by its high winds. And it gets very, very cold. A temperature of minus 100 degrees was once recorded on its perilous flanks.

This mountain is called Denali.

"Aha!" you are thinking. "This is a story about how Caroline attempted to summit Denali!" But you are wrong. I may be stupid sometimes, but I'm not that stupid. Of course I know my mountaineering skills are not up to ascending to the top of a mountain with terrible blizzards, gale-force winds, and blood-stopping temperatures. But that doesn't mean that when I was asked by my friend Eric if I wanted to visit him on Denali, where he worked as a park ranger, I was going to say no. Denali was treacherous. Very treacherous. But sometimes the word "treacherous" lacks the menace it should, and sounds strangely like the word "fun."

I arrived with my friend Trish in a small six-seater plane that smelled like it had been filled with people who hadn't showered in a month. This was because it had been filled with people who hadn't showered in a month, also known as mountain climbers. The plane landed on a makeshift snow runway at an elevation of eight thousand feet. Next to this makeshift runway was a makeshift town. A makeshift house—basically a tarpaulin pulled over some metal and wood—was the centerpiece of this town and served as tiny hospital, communications center, and, if you were lucky, hot chocolate dispenser. Otherwise, the town, also called "base camp," consisted of tents from various countries, as this was where climbers began their summit bids; and this was where Eric carried out much of his work as a park ranger. The plan was that Trish and I would pitch our own tents here, far from any danger. We would help Eric with small duties, and venture out on half-day ski forays.

It was marvelous. Everything was marvelous. Even the toilet was marvelous. It was a high-backed wooden throne, partially hidden by a snowdrift, that looked out onto majestic peaks, vast glacial plains, and even intermittent avalanches, which sluiced from far-off mountainsides with a delayed roar. If you

---

SHE SAID...

"Never give up, because that is just the place and time that the tide will change."
—**Harriet Beecher Stowe**, author, human rights activist

---

can love a toilet then I loved that toilet, and I often found it hard to remember that I was not seated there to gawk at the view.

One day soon after we arrived, the forecast for the mountain said something unexpected: It was going to be clear and balmy for the next week. Where were the terrible blizzards? Where were the high winds? Where were the blood-stopping temperatures? Gone. Suddenly Denali, with none of its fierce weather, seemed tame.

It was as if a large tiger had abruptly sighed and said, forget this, I'm going to be a kitten for a while. And what do you do with a cute cuddly kitten? You tickle its tummy and play with its nose. So suddenly we were not sticking to our plan of remaining at base camp. We were pondering a two-day expedition to the next camp at fourteen thousand feet. We asked each other: What could possibly go wrong? We asked as if it was a question, but it wasn't a question. It was a statement. The weather was fine, is what we meant, so nothing could possibly go wrong.

As you have guessed by spending this much time with me and this book, a lot could possibly go wrong. Tigers might turn into kittens, but the kittens are still very, very hungry.

It was an easy ski those first few hours. It helped that Eric had taken the first shift dragging the hundred-pound sled that held much of our supplies. But the slope was gentle, and the weather, as promised, was mild. But did I mention the crevasses? Yes, there were many, many crevasses.

A crevasse is a split in the glacier or ice layer. Some are shallow, but some descend fifteen stories or more below the surface. This was why on this beautiful day the three of us were "roped up," which meant we were tied together

---

SHE SAID...

"My favorite thing is to go where I've never been." —**Diane Arbus**, photographer

GIRL HERO!

Crina "Coco" Popescu climbed the Alps when she was eleven years old, Kala Pattar in Nepal when she was twelve, and Alam Kuh in Iran when she was thirteen. To date this Romanian teenager has summited the highest volcano and the highest mountain on each continent, a list that includes behemoths like Everest, Aconcagua, and of course, Denali.

by a long and sturdy climbing rope. This way, if one of us tumbled into a crevasse, the other two would stop the fall. If the unlucky person was unconscious or hurt, and couldn't climb up the rope herself, the other two would hoist her to the surface. There is a lot of weird math and physics involved in this hoisting, but suffice it to say that the rope was angled and staked in a way that turned it into a "leverage system"—which is a boring way to describe the boring sentence, "We were maximizing our capacity to lift, and minimizing our capacity to pull." I just called it, at various times, the Hoister, the Puller-Upper, or the Thankyouthankyouthankyou (because that's what climbers say upon reaching the surface).

I had practiced crevasse rescue just the day before. While Eric and Trish set up the Thankyouthankyouthankyou up top, I had dangled from my harness below, inside the crevasse. Around me, ice-blue walls undulated like funhouse mirrors. Under my swaying feet, the crevasse narrowed but didn't end; it continued downward, turning black as it lost light. It went for miles, I was sure, and a fall would be long, scary, and fatal. I knew that my equipment was sturdy; nevertheless I repeatedly checked my carabiners for any sign of failure and the rope for any sign of frays. I was both exhilarated and spooked.

Today, the crevasses were everywhere. The weather all summer had been unseasonably warm, and this new spell of balminess didn't help. Melting snow revealed cracks all around us. At first this was intimidating. But soon our jumpiness subsided. Most of the crevasses were narrow enough to ski over. If they weren't, we diverted from our line to find a snow bridge. Soon we weren't even that interested. Another crevasse. Yawn.

Eric stopped for the umpteenth time. "Crevasse!!" he shouted back. He was twenty-five feet from Trish, and another twenty-five feet from me (it was important to keep our rope spaced correctly). He pondered it for longer than usual.

"I'm going to jump it!" he finally yelled.

For some reason, jumping a crevasse seemed like a fine idea. After all, we'd been skiing for hours, and we'd become expert crevasse crossers. We were also tired, and getting lazy. Eric removed his skis, his poles, and his rucksack, chucking each over the crack only he could see. Then he slacked the rope attached to the one-hundred-pound sled. He walked a few steps back, put up his hand in a wave, ran forward, and jettisoned himself into the air. His arms windmilled and his legs whirred. He looked like a cartoon character jumping over a chasm.

And like most cartoon characters who jump over chasms, he disappeared.

My brain didn't register that the lip had given way just as Eric's back foot

---

GIRL HERO!

 You know what they say: Ginger Rogers did everything her famous dance partner, Fred Astaire, did, but backward and in high heels. It's true for many women adventurers, too: They forged the same rivers, climbed the same mountains, crossed the same hostile terrain as men, but they did it wearing corsets, oversize hats, ankle-length dresses, and high-heeled button boots—and riding side saddle. In 1895, **Fanny Workman** biked 2,800 miles with her husband across Spain—in a skirt. She also biked across North Africa and through India. But in 1898 she fell in love with mountaineering. Still wearing skirts and fashionable hats, she climbed peaks all around the Himalayas.

---

had pushed off from the snow. Nor did it realize that this meant Eric was falling into the crevasse. But in the next second Trish was jerked to the ground. Then the tension on the rope reached me. I was jerked to the ground.

We slid. Toward the crevasse.

WHAM. I jammed my ice axe into the snow, doing what was called a "self-arrest." A self-arrest is not when you turn yourself in at the nearest police station. It's when you take it upon yourself to stop your forward or backward slide, in many cases by using an ice axe. Frankly, I would have preferred to turn myself in at a police station. But that was not to be.

There was silence.

Silence, except for the sound that adrenaline must make as it floods the body. Silence, except for the clicking and clacking as my brain began to assess this new succession of facts. Eric, in crevasse. Trish and me, prone on snow. Ice axe, our savior.

Trish and I called to each other. Okay? Okay! Then we called for Eric.

No response.

Was he dead? Was he unconscious? We didn't know. But this was no time to lie about, even if we were lying about because gravity and more than three hundred pounds of swinging, possibly dead, weight was pulling on us. If the hundred-pound sled that had followed Eric down hadn't killed him, hypothermia would. Once the heat began to leach from Eric's body, he would have only a little time. So we had work to do, and I was the one who had to do it. It was time to set up the Thankyouthankyouthankyou, so I scrabbled for the stakes I was carrying on my back, and I drove one into the snow with the ferocity of someone aiming for a vampire's heart.

This stake was to be the anchor, which was a very important element of the Thankyouthankyouthankyou. As anchor, this stake had to hold the weight Trish and I were now holding, of Eric and his sled. Deep into the snow it went. I tied the rope to its end, then piled snow on top. Now the anchor was set. Or I hoped it was set. I pulled on it, just to make sure. To my horror, it failed, popping easily out of the soft and mushy snow.

"AAAAAAaaaarrrggghhh!" I cried.

The very weather that had made us feel so safe was now conspiring against us. The warmth that had lulled us into believing everything was going to be fine had opened up crevasses and turned the snow soft and mushy. Denali had been a friendly kitten for a while. But it remained a wild tiger at heart, and we had made the mistake of forgetting that.

I had to build a new anchor. So I grabbed all four of my stakes. I shoved them deep in the snow. It wasn't elegant, but when I pulled on the rope this anchor held.

I began to shift the load from my harness to the stakes.

Suddenly, I felt a teardrop on my face. But, hold it, I wasn't crying (yet). I looked up at the sky in disbelief. It had begun to rain. Rain! This was a mountain known for its blizzards, even in summer. How could it be raining?

The snow instantly began to melt under me. No! I unburied my stakes like a dog unburying his bone, limbs digging, snow flying. I carved out a deeper hole, dropped in my stakes, retied the rope, and piled the snow back on. New anchor! It held. Quickly I set up the rest of the system.

I shouted to Trish. The anchor was set, ready to take all the weight. The

GIRL HERO!

 Aidan Campbell was fifteen years old when she began to accompany her dad to the Arctic Circle. She spent one month every season there, for a year. She learned to build a cabin and forage for food. She endured winter temperatures of fifty degrees below zero. She hiked with pepper spray to protect herself from grizzlies. The most difficult test of all, though, came from the swarms of mosquitoes in the summer months. Among her adventures was a hike across the Brooks Range and then a treacherous canoe paddle to the Arctic Ocean.

GIRL HEROES!

World War I was winding down, but able young men were still fighting at the front, so in 1918 short-staffed Yosemite National Park reluctantly hired eighteen-year-old **Claire Marie Hodges**, who became the first female park ranger in the country. It took thirty more years to hire another full-time female ranger. **Betty Reid Soskin** is, at ninety-two, the oldest full-time park ranger in the U.S. She works at the Rosie the Riveter/World War II Home Front National Historical Park in Richmond, California, and is one of the only rangers who remembers the war effort, during which time she worked as a clerk for the black workers in the segregated boilermakers' union.

---

leverage system had been made, ready to haul Eric up. Now all we needed was for Trish to unclip from the system.

But she couldn't unclip. She was being pulled from two directions, and the pressure on the carabiner was too much. She twisted, pawed, even breathed warm air in its direction. Nothing worked. The carabiner gate wouldn't open.

"I'm stuck!" she yelled.

My heart began to race. I knew the warm rain was not only melting the snow, it was soaking Eric. Hypothermia! My breathing short and shallow, my brain addled, I shouted the only idea my overloaded neural pathways could manage.

"Take your knife and cut your harness off!" I yelled.

I'll admit it right now: This was not a good idea. You need your harness on at all times. Also, a knife around a rope was a scary thing, because you could cut the wrong part of the rope by accident. But I couldn't think of any other ideas, and it was clear we had to try something. So it was going to have to be the knife. At which point Trish yelled back at me.

"I don't have a knife!"

No knife??? Everyone knows you have to have a knife in the wilderness. You have to have it within reach and you have to have it sharp. Disbelief and

SHE SAID...

"I remembered what it was really like: crouching to pee in the woods at two a.m. while the wolves howled, baring my butt at thirty-five below . . . 'The bathroom situation,' I say. 'It's what you could call . . .' I thought for a second. 'Rustic. Yes, very rustic.'" —Teen adventurer **Aidan Campbell**, upon being asked about "the bathroom situation" during her winter month stay in the Arctic Circle

annoyance crossed over my face. But instead of saying how disbelieving and annoyed I was, I said, "I have a knife, I'll throw it to you." Now it was Trish's turn to be disbelieving and annoyed.

Trish was on the national champion Frisbee team. She knew how to throw. And she knew that I did not, because she had, on a few occasions at least, attempted to teach me to throw a Frisbee. The attempts had been a disaster. The Frisbee had careered off to one side repeatedly. Or it had dropped sadly to the ground in front of me. On one or two occasions it had even disappeared behind me.

But a knife is not a Frisbee. And I had seen enough movies to know that when a knife is tossed by the hero to someone in need, it lands exactly where it should.

So I picked up the knife, and I centered myself. "Be the hero," I whispered. I inhaled a deep breath. I brought my arm back. Exhaling, I tossed the knife.

It landed fifteen feet wide, disappearing into the snow. "AAARRRG-GHH," I yelled in disbelief.

"AAAARRRGGHH," Trish yelled, with the same vigor. This was not a movie, it turned out. This was real life and in real life I remained a nincompoop who couldn't throw a Frisbee or a knife.

We calmed down. Trish continued her efforts to take some of the pressure off the carabiner and open its gate. She crab-crawled, twisted, and pulled. Snow flew. Finally, she called out in triumph.

"I've undone it!" She was free of the loop she had been attached too. Smiling, she undid her skis and threw them in my direction. Then she clipped her carabiner back onto the main rope, slid it forward, and stood up to walk toward me.

Bad luck comes in threes, everyone knows that. There had been the fall in the crevasse, the rain, and then the badly aimed knife. Good luck was in store from now on, right? But on some occasions bad luck comes in fours, and today was such an occasion. I watched Trish's legs take a step toward me and then suddenly disappear into the snow. Her chest followed. At this point her arms shot out, and her downward movement stopped, and then Trish hung there, eyes wide, face pale, in one of those Iron Cross moves that top-notch Olympic gymnasts perform. Then she swung her legs up from inside the snow in a superhuman move that she would never, ever be able to do again. Rolling off to the side she lay spread-eagle and unmoving.

"I'm not on solid snow!" she shouted. "I've just punched through." She took a deep, deep breath. "Caroline, the crevasse is underneath me!"

Crevasses look like long, narrow cracks in the snow. But they can open up into huge looming caverns underneath. How big was this cavern? Would the snow break through anywhere else? We had no way to know. As Trish crawled toward me, trying to spread her weight as wide as possible, I wondered, Did bad luck come in fives? What I meant was: Am I on a thin layer of snow at this very moment?

Both Trish and I were tied into the anchor I had set. But would the anchor hold with the falling weight of all three of us? I doubted it. But that scenario was unthinkable, so I did what all people do when they need to concentrate on the task at hand with a clear mind and steady hand. I un-thinked it.

Trish and I began to pull on the Thankyouthankyouthankyou. It was slow going. The rope bit into the soft and mushy snow, hampering our progress immensely. We pulled and pulled, the rope sank and sank, and little by little Eric and his sled began to rise. But it was too slow, and we knew it.

Then tiny dots appeared on the horizon. The dots snaked quickly toward us, enlarging into people. It was a team of climbers, descending the mountain!

"Climbers! Descending the mountain!" Trish called out happily.

A part of me was happy, too. But a part of me was not happy. We were in the wilderness and we were in a pickle of our own making, and it was our job to get ourselves out of it. But we weren't expert mountaineers, and we weren't un-pickling ourselves, and in no time the team arrived. It consisted of a large group of amateur climbers. Their guides skied up to the crevasse. We looked at the two guides and they looked at us.

We were staring at two female mountaineers, genuine kick-ass gals, shining examples of superhero skill, and at that moment very disgusted with us. They threw us a withering look: You got yourself in this situation and you can't get yourself out? With a yawn, and a slow, stern shake of her superhero head, one of the women guides unspooled a rope from her back. She commanded her ten clients to grip that rope with their hands. Then she clipped in.

Now this seemed a little unfair. No anchor in the soft mushy snow? No Thankyouthankyouthankyou? Just the twenty hands of ten eager climbers. But I swallowed my pride and watched as the kick-ass woman guide rappelled (a technique climbers use to descend a rope) into the crevasse, while her clients held fast. We waited. Five minutes later she jugged (a technique climbers use to ascend a rope) her way back up.

"He's alive," she said in the same tone of voice you might use to say Pass the Butter, or Two Plus Two Equals Four. And why not? As a kick-ass superhero mountaineer she had seen many things, it was clear, and being alive was the most normal of them. Then she added, "But there's blood all down the walls. Let's do this fast." In the same Pass the Butter voice she commanded her clients to pull on the rope, now attached to Eric.

Eric was badly injured. He was cold and wet, and the hundred-pound sled had hit him on the head, cutting it open and knocking him unconscious. He had suffered a concussion, and the gash on his head would need eighty stitches, plus, he had fractured his back. Right now, Eric was taking small steps in the snow and looking around as if he didn't recognize where he was. We radioed in for a helicopter. The woman guides called their team to attention, then tilted their square chins at us and, in the tradition of superheroes everywhere, skied away with hardly a word.

What did I learn from this misadventure? I learned that there was a snow bridge over which to cross that crevasse just ten yards away; we had been careless, impatient, and cocky. I learned that warm weather on Denali may seem nice, but it was also unexpected. I learned that it was often the unexpected, no matter how welcome it seemed, that got you in trouble. I learned that Trish and I hadn't saved Eric's life, but we hadn't killed him either. I learned that a concussion, fractured vertebrae, and eighty stitches are serious medical issues but with the right care a person as tough as Eric can recover just fine. I learned that bad luck can come in fours, which probably means it can come in fives, sixes, and sevens. I learned that good luck appears in the guise of two disgusted mountaineer women. I learned that superheroes are real, even if they aren't very friendly. I learned that treacherous can mean fun, but I wasn't to forget that it means treacherous, too.

DERRING-DO
STAY WARM

You're outside and starting to shiver. Stuff your clothes with dry leaves, small twigs, and moss! Why? The air spaces trap heat, just like the light loft in your favorite winter coat (but if you're inside and starting to shiver, um, turn up the heat). Balled up newspaper and book pages also work (maps too, but only if you know exactly where you are and don't need them). Avoid hypothermia at all costs!

Try this: Put on some old clothes. Stuff paper, dry leaves, and twigs into your shirt and pants. Yes, you look silly. But you're silly and warm (and safe!)

DERRING-DO

ESTIMATE THE TIME BEFORE SUNDOWN!

You're on an outdoor expedition. You want to set up your campsite before dark. But you left your watch at home. Use your fingers!

Try this: Reach forward until both your arms are straight. Bend your hands inward at the wrist, fingers touching, so that your palms face you. Now you're ready: position one hand at the horizon, with thumb down against palm (thumbs don't count here.) Stack the other hand on top, thumb dropped, and keep doing this until you reach the sun. Each finger is about fifteen minutes. If you have stacked two hands/eight fingers, it's two hours until sundown. Now check your result with the real time. NOTE: Finger size will vary!

FINGER TIME

DERRING-DO

FIND WATER!

Physical activities like skiing, hiking, and rescuing friends from crevasses require hydration. But sometimes drinking water is not so readily available (i.e., sometimes the hiking canteen is mistakenly left behind by someone. Not mentioning any names, but the initials may be "C" and "P"). Learn to collect drinking water in the outdoors!

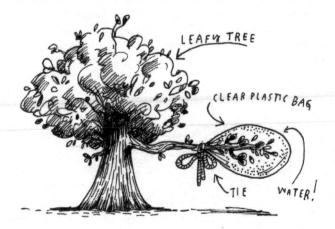

LEAFY TREE

CLEAR PLASTIC BAG

TIE

WATER!

Try this: Pull a clear plastic garbage bag onto a leafy tree branch or bush (make sure it isn't a poisonous plant!), then seal it as best you can by tying its end against the branch. When the sun hits the branch the leaves will begin to perspire water, in a process called transpiration. Water will collect in the lowest part of the garbage bag. If no branches are available put handfuls of green leaves and grass into the bag instead. NOTE: Black garbage bags don't allow the sunlight to penetrate to the branch. Only clear plastic bags let sunlight in, triggering the photosynthesis process and, in turn, transpiration.

JOURNAL THIS!

What adventures and goals do you have for the future? Write a Life List! (Here are some Life List entries from real adventurers: ride in a balloon, act in a Tarzan movie, raft the Nile, build a telescope, land on and take off from an aircraft carrier, bivouac in a tree, visit the moon . . .) Don't worry if they seem impossible. Just write them down!

CHAPTER 6

IT'S PITCH DARK, BUT YOU CAN STILL FIND YOUR WAY

THERE ARE MANY things I describe as "fun." Tickling someone as they juggle four uncooked eggs, for example. Or guessing the number of jelly beans in a jar, winning, and eating all the jelly beans. Also, puppies. Anything that involves puppies! And throwing cooked lasagna noodles at the wall hoping they stick.

But searching for a dead body is not my idea of fun, especially when that

dead body is somewhere in the cold, murky bay water into which I was now peering.

But fun or not, I was wearing fins, mask, wet suit, and scuba gear. I was floating in my inflated vest and waiting for the uniformed man on the dock to give me an order. The uniformed man on the dock was my officer in the San Francisco Fire Department, where I was a firefighter and trained SCUBA diver. Searching for bodies was part of my job. Not my idea of fun, but definitely my idea of adventure.

The body had been missing for a day or even two, and this was both bad news and good news and bad news again. The bad news was that a body in the water for that long begins to succumb to fish, which like to feast on the eyes, and to the ravages of water, which bloat the body and peel off the skin. The good news was that the tides and currents were so fierce in this part of the bay, there was a good chance the body was long gone. The bad news was that if the body was long gone, the family would be even more sad than they were and, for me as a rescue diver, this was intolerable. So as my officer tugged on the rope I was holding, signaling me to begin my descent into the cold, dark water, I made a wish that I would find the body. I also wished for that body to contain both of its eyes and all of its skin. Genies gave out three wishes all the time; these two seemed fair enough.

GIRL HERO!

 Erika Bergman is a submersible (aka submarine) pilot and National Geographic Young Explorer. She drives to depths of two thousand feet in a steel compartment that has to withstand seventy times the pressure we feel on land. The strangest sight she's ever seen? At eighteen hundred feet below the surface, a twenty-foot Siphono-phore, which looked like one very large caterpillar, but she says was actually made up of many, many tiny creatures. Erika is currently part of Team Sedna, a group of intrepid young women who will snorkel across the Arctic in 2016.

I began to deflate my vest, allowing myself to slowly sink. The water was a lightish brown. As I descended it blackened. I could hear my breath in my ears, but otherwise it was as if I'd fallen into a wormhole, and I was inexplicably tumbling through the universe, sightless, weightless, completely alone. It was so dark I couldn't see my hand in front of my face. I kept dropping, and then I felt mud against my exposed cheeks. Had I finally reached the bottom?

Not yet. I had enough experience in these waters to know that a three-foot layer of silt covered the floor of the bay. So I couldn't stop here. I had to get to the bottom of the bottom, and this meant sinking all the way into the mud, then flattening out and letting that mud cover me. I dropped a little more, then felt the hard, packed sand. The bottom! I was here.

What must I have looked like to an all-seeing sea creature at that moment? The mud would have been swirling around me. I was stretched out like a skydiver, neutrally buoyant, as the dive lingo goes, my stomach brushing the bay floor. There may have been a hint of light emanating from my shoulder, but it was only evident to me if I put my eye right up to the flashlight attached there, and then only as a bleary, brown halo. How was I going to spot a body, you ask (or maybe you didn't ask, but I'm going to tell you), in such desperate gloom?

GIRL HERO!

 Cristina Zenato grew up in the African Congo. She became an accomplished diver and, soon, a "shark whisperer." Cristina calms sharks by rubbing around the animal's nose and mouth, along small jelly-filled holes called the Ampullae of Lorenzini. This quiets the shark into a semi-paralytic state, for up to twenty minutes. During that time Cristina pulls fishhooks from their mouths, removes parasites from their hides, and extracts their DNA for research. She calls sharks "the most maligned and misunderstood creatures, and a crucial component to our ocean ecosystem . . . Some call [sharks] man's most feared predator. I just call them family."

GIRL HERO!

In 1926, **Gertrude Ederle** swam the English Channel. She was twenty years old. It took her fourteen hours and thirty-one minutes, but she smashed the former record (set by a man) by two hours. She was only the sixth person to complete the Channel swim and she succeeded on her second attempt (perseverance!). She hit heavy seas and stormy weather. Even her coach tried to persuade her to quit. "It could be done, it had to be done, and I did it," she said of the crossing.

The answer is, I wouldn't spot the body. But I would feel the body. Yes, I was going to search the floor of the bay using my hands.

I told myself that nothing down here could hurt me—there were no blood-thirsty sharks, no murderous humans; and monsters did not exist. Or did they? Floating in the pitch black, it was easy to believe that gremlins, goblins, eight-headed eels, or underwater yetis were lurking nearby. Through force of will I banished these thoughts. Then I banished the image of a body with vacant eye sockets and billowing skin. In its place I stuck an image of a plaid shirt. Plaid shirts weren't scary, even if the bodies in them were. Good. I was now ready.

Then someone's finger ran up my leg.

What???!! Another brushed along my back. Fingers? It couldn't be. I exhaled, controlling my surprise and potential panic. My imagination, surely. There was no one here. No one with moving hands, that was for sure.

SHE SAID...

"All over the green and brown bits [of earth] we draw lines, we claim nations . . . [then] I meet pods of dolphins . . . who carry no passports, have no allegiance, and look pretty damn happy for it." —**Hanli Prinsloo**, freediver, who can hold her breath underwater for six minutes, and who swims with whales, sharks, and rays around the world, wearing no SCUBA gear

GIRL HERO!

Sylvia "Her Deepness" Earle is an oceanographer and explorer. She has spent a total of a year of her life underwater! It was not easy at first. In the 1960s marine expeditions refused Earle's participation, despite her extensive experience, because she was a woman. But she persisted and has since led many underwater explorations. In 1986, she dove solo in a submarine to one thousand meters, tying the world record at the time.

Or was there?

Naaah. I wouldn't let my imagination take over. I had a job to do. I wasn't about to be a scaredy-cat now.

But, wait, there it was again. More fingers now, scurrying, darting, scrabbling, scribbling across my wet suit.

Crabs. Swarming crabs.

It was a strange feeling, but not too scary after the initial shock, maybe even a little comforting, because now I knew I wasn't alone down here. I took a few slow breaths and stayed still, getting used to the tiny, strange feet. After a few moments, my heart had slowed, and I felt relaxed again. I'm good, they're good, let's start this thing, I thought to myself. I rustled one fin slightly and then the other. I propelled myself slowly, slowly, slowly forward and began sweeping my free hand from side to side.

CRAB!   TAKE-OUT!

SHE SAID...

"If you're never scared, or embarrassed, or hurt, it means you aren't taking any chances." —**Julia Sorel**, artist

---

I still couldn't see anything, but by pure touch alone, the bay floor took shape. Pipes, bottles, a shopping cart. I hit a tire. A plastic bag wrapped around my hand. Sometimes my fingers closed on something I didn't recognize—a shoe?—and I just dropped it back into the silt. The crabs continued to scurry over me. I got used to the darkness, the whoosh of my respirator in my ear, the light pressure of the silt. I forgot I had no vision. The bottom began to materialize slowly, like a ship appearing from the fog. Bottles jutted up from the sand. Shopping cart wheels spun in the current. Crawdads and fish peeked out from behind slabs of discarded concrete and rebar, and here and there a lobster curious about the large pendulous shadow swimming toward her, waved a claw in tepid self-defense.

But of course this was nonsense. My brain was tricking me. It was still pitch black, the water dense with mud. I couldn't see a thing. Three sudden tugs on the rope I was holding jostled me from my reverie.

Surface, the rope was saying.

Already? How much time had passed? The body hadn't been found!

I began my slow ascent, imagining the crabs falling off me one by one, the mud parting, the stir of my fins rustling errant shoes and pushing bottles over. The blackness turned to dark brown. Then, sunlight.

SHE SAID...

"It's like having a fully grown bull balanced on one hoof on every single square inch of our small protective sphere." —**Erika Bergman**, submersible pilot, describing the water pressure that her submarine must withstand

The safety diver on the surface gave me the thumbs up. My officer gestured. I swam toward him with the awkward strokes particular to divers in full gear: part fish, part excited Labrador retriever. I grabbed the dock. I didn't want my adventure to be over. But when I looked at my air gauge I realized I had been down much longer than I had thought. It was easy to lose yourself, I realized, in the pitch black.

"We're calling it," my officer said. "With these currents . . . " He shrugged. His expression finished the sentence for him. *The body's gone.*

The lesson? Sometimes you don't find what you're looking for. You find instead you can overcome your fear of bodies with no eyes. You find you can stay calm as crabs crawl all over you. You find that pitch black has shape and feel.

My officer reaches for my fins.

"Good job," he says, and I grab the ladder to clamber out.

DERRING-DO
POWER SENTENCES!

Rita Pierson is an educator who tells students who want more confidence to say to themselves, "I am Somebody . . . I am powerful and I am strong . . . I have things to do and people to impress and places to go!" She says of this mantra, "If you say it long enough, it starts to be part of you." What's the sentence you're going to tell yourself day in and day out?

Try this: Repeat the sentence Ms. Pierson designed right now. Say it clearly! Add emphatic hand movements! Jump up and down if you want to. If you don't want anyone else to hear, that's fine, too—find a private place right now and whisper a few times. If this sentence doesn't feel completely right for you, design a sentence just for yourself, one that will empower you throughout the day no matter how many math tests you have to pass. (Don't forget the Wonder Woman Stance in Chapter 2 for an extra boost!)

DERRING-DO

FOCUS! (AND I'M NOT TALKING ABOUT CAMERAS.)

 We've all been told to "Focus!" by teachers in class. But what does it really mean? Focus is the ability to concentrate on what's most relevant in the moment, and forget the other stuff, and it can come in handy. Say you're crossing over a river full of alligators, on a rickety, slippery bridge. The alligators might be an important detail. But what's more important is walking across the bridge without slipping. Your focus must be on each step, and not on the gnashing teeth below you!

Try this: Sit in a chair. Set an egg timer for three minutes. Take a breath in through your nose, expanding your belly as you do so. Notice your breath, how it feels, how it sounds. If your mind wanders to your homework (sure), or food (yup), bring your attention gently back to your breathing. Now exhale. Listen to the sound, pay attention to how it feels. Keep breathing, and paying attention to your breathing. You will think of other things, too—that's okay, just direct yourself back to your breath. When the egg timer goes off, pat yourself on the back. If you can't reach, ask someone else to. You deserve it! You focused!

JOURNAL THIS!

Write down the areas in which you are really confident (your knock-knock jokes? The love of your dog? Your compass reading abilities?) Now pick a separate area in which you want to gain confidence (saying hi first, answering questions in class, climbing a tree, fixing your bike tire). Write "I want to gain confidence in . . . " and fill in the blank. Here's the cool part: accomplishing something important entails a series of small steps, nothing big! The first step is setting the goal, which is what you're doing here.

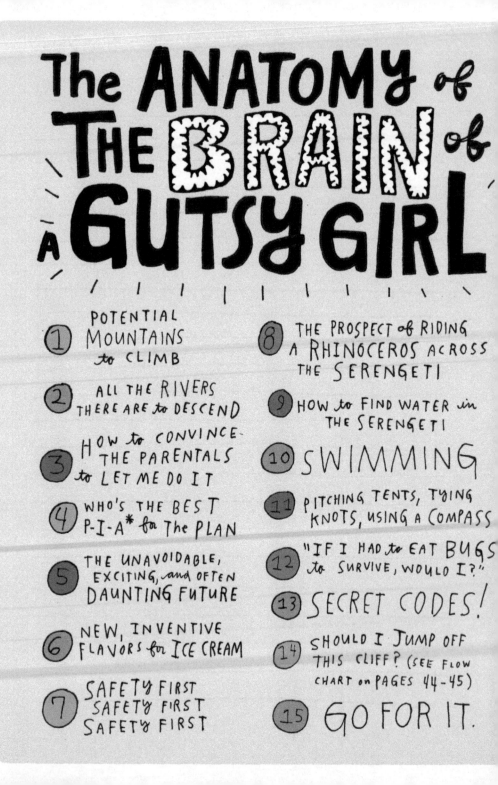

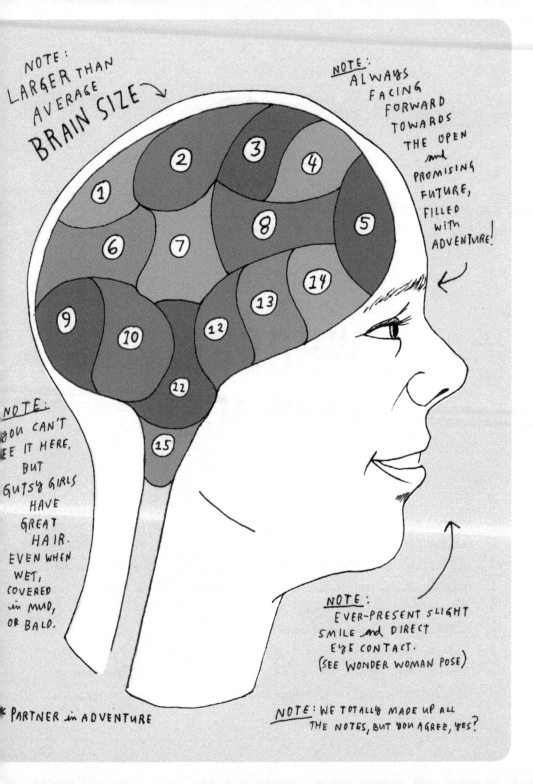

CHAPTER 7

WHOOPS! THIN ICE!

WHEN I WAS your age (not so short ago, but not so long ago either), I wanted very badly to compete in the Olympics. But how? I was of average height and weight. I couldn't jump high or run fast. My balance was so-so. My hand-eye coordination was terrible. But what if I trained for an athletic endeavor that few people competed in? Then I'd have a chance.

Welcome to the obscure sport of Luge.

How obscure? There was only one place in the whole country at which to train (the U.S. Olympic Training Center in Lake Placid, New York). Almost all of the members of the U.S. luge team were born and raised in one town (the town of Lake Placid). Only a few women in the whole country competed. Hurrah! Clearly this was the sport for me.

Luge is similar to sledding down a hill on a cafeteria tray. But instead of calling it sledding it's called sliding, instead of a hill there's an ice track, instead of a cafeteria tray there's a carbon fiber aerodynamically shaped sled, and instead of mittens, a hat, and a puffy coat, there's a skintight polyester racing suit and a helmet. But other than all that, it's exactly like sledding down a hill on a cafeteria tray.

Olympians from all over the world practiced on the Lake Placid luge track. Every day they gathered at the starting hut, keeping warm, making friends, waiting their turn, and there I was, a rank beginner, milling among these formidable athletes. "Rodelbahn!" a voice would then shout over a scratchy loudspeaker, clearing the track as a luger set her sled at the starting line. A countdown in German would commence. (Many race-related announcements were in German, because the sport began in Switzerland. The Swiss also speak French, from which the word "luge"—sled—comes. They speak Italian and Romansh, too, but no words from these languages appear in the sport, except perhaps "Mama Mia!" which may be exclaimed after a particularly bad crash.)

GIRL HERO!

 To the local Sherpa men, summiting Mount Everest was a sacred act. **Pasang Lhamu** decided it was high time a woman joined them. She became the first female Sherpa to climb to the top of the mountain her people called Chomolongma, the Mother Goddess of the Universe. Breaking from deep-rooted traditions that kept women to the home and fields, Lhamu first attempted Everest, without oxygen, in 1990. Weather forced her to turn around only eight hundred meters from the top. She finally summited in 1993, but she died in an avalanche on the way down. She became a national heroine and an inspiration to Nepali women. An all-women Sherpa team summited Everest in 2000.

The luger pushed herself off. She hurtled down the track: fast, faster, fastest! There would be no braking, but there were many ways to stop, most of them unwanted, like flipping over, or skidding sideways, or being ejected from the sled during a particularly tight turn and hitting the wall. Steering was done with your legs, which pressed against the runners. Minute movements of the head and shoulders also helped maneuver. Speeds reached ninety miles per hour. Once past the finish line you slammed your feet onto the ice and pulled up on the runners with your hands. Ice and snow flying, you finally skittered to a halt.

There are many cool nicknames to have when you're a luger. "Speedy" comes to mind. "The Bullet" would be nice. How about "Top Dawg"? Unfortunately, my nickname was "Crash."

The problem was Curve 10. It was a nasty corkscrew turn that liked to flick a luge sled onto its side the same way you would flick an ant off your jelly sandwich. Specifically, it liked to flick MY luge sled on its side. You would think this would have put a dent in my Olympic dream. But this did not deter me.

THE TRACK

Perhaps it should have. I began to crash often and with spectacular twisty-turny-flippy moves worthy of a circus acrobat. At different times I hit my shoulders, my head, my feet. Once I was taken to the hospital by ambulance, where I was diagnosed with injured ribs and questionable judgment. (Just

GIRL HERO!

 Farhana Huq didn't start surfing until she was twenty-six. Her first day on the waves was embarrassing and difficult. But a few years later she decided to try again. Soon she was hooked! She decided to spread her newfound passion to areas where girls were not traditionally encouraged to surf. She founded Brown Girl Surf, which strives to connect female surfers from around the world, and encourages girls to take on waves in India, Bangladesh, Sri Lanka, and beyond!

kidding. "Questionable judgment" was not an official diagnosis. But it was definitely something that the nurses and doctors pondered.)

Just a few weeks after I'd arrived at the Lake Placid Olympic Training Center, the Luge National Championships were held. The day was bitterly cold and terribly windy. I was a beginner, and my nickname was Crash, but of course I signed up to race. There were twelve entrants. Perfect! The worst that could happen was that I would be ranked the twelfth best luger in the country.

One by one the lugers raced. One by one those who crossed the finish line changed into winter gear, huddled together, and watched their fellow racers flash by. But as the day wore on these lugers decided that it was getting much too bitterly cold and terribly windy. "Let's go inside!" one whined, just as the announcer called my name. "Not yet! It's Crash!" someone shouted excitedly. The group ran to Curve 10, suddenly willing to endure the bitter cold and terrible winds. They wanted to see what grotesque punishment physics, gravity, and the corkscrew turn of Curve 10 had in store for me.

And crash I did. It was beautiful in its way. My sled and I ricocheted off the bank and somersaulted. Midair, we parted ways. Once back on the ice we both spun like a top; I still had the sled by my fingertips, but that was all. Freed of my inept steering, the sled now careened toward the finish line with a mind of its own. I was right behind, belly on the ice, holding on.

This was all that was necessary to avoid disqualification. I slid, bumped, and crawled across the finish line, becoming the 11th best luger in the country, or as I liked to later put it, "In the top eleven." (My memory fails me but I think the 12th person either dropped out or was disqualified.)

I remained at the Lake Placid Training Center for the full season. I trained hard. I crashed less spectacularly. But gradually I began to concede: Maybe I would never make it to the Olympics.

But.

It just so happened that an even more obscure sport was training nearby, on a second Lake Placid track. This sport was called Skeleton. It was a scary name for a sport, but it described the slim frailty of the sled and not, as I thought, the fate of its rider. Skeleton was similar to luging. Instead of sliding on her back feet first, a skeleton rider lay on her stomach, headfirst, and instead of a skintight polyester suit and helmet she wore jeans and a motorcycle helmet, and instead of a luge ice track, she shared the track with the bobsledders. But other than all that, it was exactly like luging.

I say "she," to describe the skeleton rider, but there were no women on the skeleton team. None at all. Nada. Zero. Zilch.

Yes, you guessed it.

I saw my chance.

I walked from the luge track to the skeleton track. I asked for the captain, and introduced myself to a tall, pale, appropriately bony (skeleton-y) white guy in jeans and Converse sneakers. He held his motorcycle helmet in one hand and the sled that looked like a cafeteria tray in the other.

"I'd like to try the skeleton," I told him.

He lit up. So few people were interested in his sport; skeleton was underfunded, understaffed, and underknown. He would be thrilled to teach such a skilled and competent luger and happy to have me on his team. It wasn't an Olympic sport yet, he added, but it would be soon.

"Soon" sounded good to me.

Just then we heard the shushing of runners on ice. The captain turned to me and said, "Let's watch Mike take this turn." Next thing I knew there was a vicious scraping sound, and a high-pitched scream. Mike whizzed by.

"Was that a scream?" I asked.

The captain shrugged. "Mike always does that," he said. "The g-forces on this turn are really wild. His face slams into the ice. The face piece on his helmet takes most of the force, though. Don't worry."

Worry? Ha! My nickname was Crash. I had hit the ice in every conceivable way. What was a little freezer burn on the chin to me?

"Will you give me a lesson?" I asked, nodding at the sled in the captain's hand and then back at the track.

"Lesson?" The captain looked puzzled. "Just lie on the sled face first. Then steer with your toes against the track. That's all you need to know."

He handed me his sled and his motorcycle helmet and motioned for me to follow him up the hill.

It's good to face problems, bullies, and facts. But it's a whole different story

GIRL HERO!

 Lynne Cox is a swimmer who likes her water cold. She once swam five miles of the Bering Strait, in a temperature of 38 degrees Fahrenheit (to get a sense of how cold that is, remember that fresh water freezes at 32 degrees.) She has twice held the record (male or female) for the fastest crossing of the English Channel. She swam a mile in Antarctica. She also tackled the 28.8 degree ocean (salt water freezes at 28.4 degrees Fahrenheit) off of Greenland, becoming the first to survive such low temperatures, let alone swim in them for five minutes and 26 seconds! She has been extensively studied by the military and by academic researchers, who remain mostly baffled by her ability to withstand such dangerous temperatures. "There is no limit to the human body," she says.

SHE SAID...

"This girl is the best thing since food."—**Mamie "Peanut" Johnson**, as she watched twelve-year-old baseball sensation **Mo'ne Davis** pitch a shutout (4-0) in the 2014 Little League World Series. Ms. Peanut Johnson was the first professional female baseball pitcher ever, and one of only three other women who played in the segregated Negro League from 1953 to 1956. Her career of thirty-three wins and eight losses against rival all-male teams speaks for itself!

to face a steep downhill, at great speed, with your chin just inches from the cold, hard ice. This was what occurred to me as I crouched by the sled and peered at the twisting chute below me. But I wasn't as nervous as I should have been. In fact, I was pretty confident. What could be worse than Curve 10? Nothing.

I pushed off as instructed and dropped belly first onto the moving sled. I shot down the track, dragging a toe around the curves, fishtailing into the straightaways. I wasn't going fast enough to encounter g-forces, so my chin skin remained intact. The only scream that emitted from me was a whoop of joy, as I crossed the finish line (on my sled!), exhilarated. I loved it.

"You're a natural!" the captain shouted happily.

Really? Me, a natural?

It was set. I would be a skeleton rider.

But.

The captain said I had to speak to the president of the Bobsled Association to join, because this was unprecedented. There were no women on any skeleton team in the world. I would be the first.

The first! I liked the sound of this very much.

"Go in the afternoon," the captain advised me. The bobsled president liked a whiskey or two around then. He'd be more approachable, he told me.

I was unsure what the fuss was about, but I knocked on the bobsled president's office door the next afternoon. He was a stout, balding man behind a large desk, who motioned me to sit down and then laughed a hearty, slightly mean laugh when I informed him why I was there.

"You can't be on the skeleton team," he said.

"Why?" I answered, puzzled.

"You just can't," he said.

"I don't understand."

"No," he said.

"But—"

"Look, you're a GIRL. We don't allow girls in the bobsled association."

"But I'm talking about the skeleton team."

"Yes, no girls there, too. They're under the bobsled association."

"But why?" I was truly baffled. I had never been told I couldn't do something because I was a girl. People had thought it in their heads perhaps, but no one had ever said it out loud.

"You're a girl, that's why."

"But—"

"NO GIRLS. That's that."

The whiskey wasn't softening him. But it was making him talkative. You see, it was illegal to bar someone from a sport for being a girl. I knew that. He probably knew that. So saying it out loud was not only mean, and illogical, but it put him immediately in legal hot water.

I had seen enough cop shows to know what to say next. "You'll hear from my lawyer," I sniffed, rising from my chair. I didn't have a lawyer, of course. But I would find one. I put my hands on my hips, tossed my head like I'd seen on TV, and marched out.

The skeleton captain was disappointed when I told him the news. He shook his head in disgust. "I had a feeling it would go like this," he said. "But I'm sorry, I can't let you on the track again until it's sorted out." I was crestfallen, but I understood. There were only a few weeks left in the training season for

SHE SAID...

"Ever since I was a child, when someone tells me I can't do something, it just empowers me all the more. People's doubts in my ability only strengthens my resolve." —**Kira Salak**, solo traveler, adventurer

all of us, anyway. Soon I would be returning home to California, and college.

I knew it would be a long drawn-out fight, and I had an Olympic dream to pursue. I turned my attention from the sport of skeleton back to the sport of luge. I learned German that summer. I traveled to a European luge track in the autumn to train on my own. Then, finally, I qualified for the U.S.A. Luge National Team.

An Olympic dream is beautiful. But dreams change. I had been determined, and stubborn, and resilient, and after much work and focus, I had been asked to join the national team. This was one step away from being an Olympian. I thought long and hard. Did I want to narrow my days to an ice track and a sled? Did I really want a life dedicated to medals and split seconds? By now I had traveled, met many different people, and become interested in things beyond just competitive sports. Surprising even myself, I decided to say no to the national team. I would set new goals, and dream new dreams, but they would no longer include the Olympics.

Was this a failure? In a certain sense, yes. I didn't become an Olympic athlete. But I did become something else. I was now someone who had hobnobbed with athletes from around the world. I had ricocheted down a luge track at high speeds. I had learned that hanging on by my fingertips no matter what paid off. I had improved bit by bit. I had qualified for the national team. I had been one of the first women in the world to throw myself onto a skeleton sled and shoot headfirst down its track. I had hired a lawyer and he had written a scathing letter. I had stood up to a small-minded man and his small-minded institution in my own small but powerful way. Perhaps I had even started the sled sliding toward a future where girls join skeleton teams. I had followed a dream and it had enriched my life. It hadn't turned out the way I thought I wanted it to, but it had turned out just the way it should.

There is a small postscript to this story. In 2002, I turned on my television and discovered that skeleton had finally become an Olympic sport. There, wearing skintight polyester racing suits, clutching fancy helmets, and holding sleds that still looked like cafeteria trays, were the members of the U.S.A. Men's Skeleton National Team. Next to them, were the proud, smiling members of—you guessed it—the U.S.A. Women's Skeleton National Team.

DERRING-DO
STAND UP TO YOUR INNER MEANIE

You tell yourself crazy things, like "I'm ugly," or "I'll never be able to do that," or "I'm stupid." Here's a tip: If you wouldn't let someone say such things to your best friend, don't let yourself say them to yourself either. Stand up to your inner meanie!

Try this: There were certainly times when my inner voice said "You can't luge, so give up now!" and it made me feel lousy and insecure. Next time you feel lousy or insecure, isolate what you are telling yourself. Write it down, and then write three reasons why the statement is not true.

Here are mine:

Inner Voice: You can't luge.

Me: I'm here in Lake Placid, aren't I?

People laugh at my crashes but they respect my resilience.

I'm the eleventh best female luger in the country, Inner Meanie!

DERRING-DO

VISUALIZE SUCCESS

Here's a strange scientific fact: You can practice running a cross-country course by imagining yourself doing it! Why? Visualizing a physical task sends brain signals to your muscles that are identical to the signals sent when actually performing the task. Isn't that weird? But so cool! Sounds perfect for lazy people, but in fact great athletes of all sorts practice visualization. It trains their brains to work more efficiently, and their bodies to respond automatically. Lugers use visualization because in fast sports that demand precise, split-second reactions, it's helpful to slow the race down and learn each movement and upcoming curve in your head. A luger may race three times in one day on a real track, but race ten more times on the same track in her head.

Try this: Pick a sport that you want to excel in. Lie on the floor and and imagine yourself performing various skills perfectly. Be very detailed! If you are throwing a ball, feel the way your shoulder twists and turns, the stitching against your fingers, the furrow of your brow. If you're swimming, marvel at the way the water splashes, and the strength in each stroke. See yourself moving with confidence and ease. If you want to add an image of yourself jumping up and down as you win the game/race/set, go ahead.

DERRING-DO
FIGURE OUT THE TEMPERATURE OUTSIDE!

You can't find a thermometer, but luckily you live somewhere with crickets.

Try this: Count the number of times a cricket chirps in fifteen seconds. Add forty. This is the outside temperature! If you don't live somewhere with crickets, and still can't find a thermometer, just put your head outside! If your breath comes out steamy, your eyelids freeze shut, and icicles block your way, the temperature is officially Too Darn Cold.

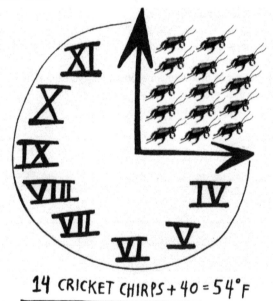

14 CRICKET CHIRPS + 40 = 54°F

NOTE: THOUGH THESE CRICKETS LOOK LIKE A TERRIFYING ARMY, THEY ARE, in FACT, QUITE SWEET INSECTS. UNLESS YOU'RE SCARED of BUGS, in WHICH CASE ADD THAT to YOUR LIST of THINGS to GET GUTSY ABOUT.

JOURNAL THIS!

Do you have a big dream, something you want to accomplish but seems too daunting? Here's a tip: break your goal into a series of smaller steps. Let's say you want to climb the tallest tree in the park:

1. Do five pushups and five pullups every day.

2. Climb ten feet up a much smaller tree.

3. Look out a window to the ground (but don't lean out too far) to get used to heights.

4. Climb fifteen feet up another tree.

5. Convince my parents I need new sneakers.

See how every steps seems manageable (except maybe the last one)? Soon you'll be ready for the really tall tree!

Try this: Use the space below to write one goal and then a list of steps that will help accomplish that goal.

CHANGE YOUR BIKE TIRE CHECKLIST:

- ✓ HOLE in TIRE.
- ○ PATCH KIT and A TIRE LEVER.
- ○ PATIENCE
- ○ CANDY (for ENERGY and MORALE)
- ○ REMOVE WHEEL (THERE IS A QUICK RELEASE LEVER on EITHER SIDE of THE FORK)
- ○ LET THE REST of THE AIR OUT of THE TIRE by PRESSING on THE VALVE with YOUR FINGER.
- ○ POSITION THE WHEEL on THE GROUND. PUSH ONE TIRE LEVER UNDER THE TIRE and PRY THE TIRE OVER THE RIM.
- ○ BE CAREFUL NOT to DAMAGE THE TUBE INSIDE.
- ○ RUN THE TIRE LEVEL ALONG THE RIM. THIS PULLS OUT THE REST of THE TIRE.
- ○ PULL OUT THE TUBE!
- ○ EAT SOME CANDY (YOU DESERVE IT!)
- ○ FIND THE HOLE. IF YOU CAN'T SEE IT, YOU CAN PUT AIR BACK in THE TIRE, SUBMERGE IT UNDERWATER and SPOT THE AIR BUBBLES.

- ⊚ PATCH IT! ROUGH UP THE AREA WITH SANDPAPER. REMOVE DIRT. APPLY THE GLUE. WAIT 3 MINUTES!

- ⊚ UNPEEL A PATCH from ITS BACKING and PRESS IT ONTO GLUE.

- ⊚ PUT THE TIRE BACK ON! PUMP A LITTLE BIT of AIR into THE TUBE. FIT IT into THE TIRE. THEN PUT THE VALVE HALFWAY into ITS HOLE on THE RIM. PUT ONE SIDE of THE TIRE (with TUBE INSIDE) on RIM and USE TIRE LEVER to PULL THE OTHER SIDE ON. THIS IS HARD at FIRST, BUT YOU'LL GET THE HANG of IT. ONCE THE TOUGH SIDE IS ON, CONTINUE INCH by INCH, UNTIL THE TIRE IS in PLACE.

- ⊚ MORE CANDY.

- ⊚ CAREFULLY MANEUVER THE VALVE FULLY THROUGH ITS HOLE.

- ⊚ INFLATE!
  PUMP SLOWLY and CAREFULLY to MAKE SURE THE TIRE IS POSITIONED CORRECTLY and WON'T PINCH A NEW HOLE.

- ⊚ CELEBRATE by DOING A "I FIXED MY TIRE" DANCE.

- ⊚ MORE CANDY.

CHAPTER 8

IT'S NOT WHAT
YOU SAY,
IT'S WHAT YOU DO

SUMMER WAS APPROACHING, school would soon let out. I needed a summer job. I knew I didn't want to work behind a desk. I wanted to be outdoors. So I decided: white-water rafting guide. I knew nothing about rivers, unless you counted the ill-fated voyage of the HMS *Homogenized*, which I did not. But I could learn. A friend mentioned a rafting company he had heard of; I found the phone number, called, and told the owner that I would be an excellent white-water employee. "I'm a competitive rower," I said, as if experience in a long thin boat carrying nine people and eight oars on very flat water were the perfect qualification for guiding on white water. It wasn't. But he must have been hard of hearing, or desperate, because he hired me.

The rafting company was very small—only seven guides total. My instruction was informal; it consisted of rafting the river a few times with an experienced guide at the helm, and then navigating the white water myself under that experienced guide's watchful eye and bellowing voice. Slowly I learned what all river guides needed to know: how to slice tomatoes and cheese and lay out bread for the customers' lunch; how to smile patiently, even when a customer asks why he can't see the tracks under the water ("Tracks?" I asked, not understanding. "Yes, the tracks this boat is on," he answered, "Like at Disney World."); and how to read a rapid, which would mean I could peer at the river and decipher the best course through its treacherous waters. At first reading a rapid was like reading someone's mind; there was a lot of intense staring on my part, and then guesswork. But soon it became similar to reading a book; I tracked my path down the white water according to the eddies, rocks, and hydraulics, scanning the rapid for the story it told of my future safe passage.

I only guided for one summer, but that experience led to rivers in remote

---

GIRL HERO!

The first person to survive Niagara Falls in a barrel was **Annie Taylor**. Desperate for money, and certain such a bold venture would gain her fame and fortune, she designed her own barrel and in 1901, in front of thousands of spectators, floated over the falls. The sixty-three-year-old survived, but after the initial excitement few took interest in someone who looked more like a grandmother than a hero. It took ten years for someone to repeat the feat; sadly, that man toured the world to wide acclaim while Annie Taylor was forgotten. But sexism couldn't hide the truth forever, and today Annie is celebrated as a gutsy adventurer and the first person over Niagara Falls.

places around the world. One of those remote places was Siberia.

Siberia? Dimly, the name rung a bell. I had heard of Siberian tigers. The Trans-Siberian railway sounded familiar. Teachers had mentioned Siberian prisons, called gulags, but always in the shuddering tones that accompany discussions of sewage systems, dead bodies, and canned spinach. Tigers, trains, prisons. None of that sounded very tantalizing. But I also knew that Siberia was vast and wild (Siberia is so huge that it takes only ten Siberias to cover all the countries on earth). It had rivers that sprang from high mountains and plummeted to the flat plains below. It had few people, and few cities. It had a night sky that glittered with a clarity seen hardly anywhere else on earth. Tigers, trains, and prisons were forgotten. I wanted to travel to this mysterious landscape, and my chance arrived in the form of a Russian-American white water expedition heading to the Altai Mountains.

These Russians lived here in Siberia. Most spoke a little English, but a few spoke none at all. Inversely, a few of the Americans spoke Russian, but most of us spoke none at all. It worked fine. We made our way through breakfasts and lunches like mimes. There's a lot you can say with smiles, nods, waving hands, and farting noises. (Just kidding about the farting noises. But wouldn't that be fun to throw in there?)

The adventure began with a five-day hike through the Altai Mountains, toward the headwaters of the Sumulta River. I noticed right away that the Russians possessed no fancy equipment. While I donned layers of sweat-wicking,

GIRL HERO!

Maya Gabeira is a big-wave surfer. How big are her big waves? Oh, about fifty feet. That's the height of a five-story building. Just saying.

GIRL HEROES!

The first descent of the Po Chu river in Bhutan was accomplished by white water kayakers **Buffy Bailey Burge**, **Maria Noakes**, and **Polly Green**. Rad!

---

thermally adjusted shirts made out of material I couldn't spell, Nadia wore one wool sweater. I slid my feet into sturdy, waterproof hiking boots with grooved soles and Velcro straps; Ivan wore flip-flops. I packed a lightweight tent with collapsible poles, mosquito netting, and way too many zippers; Vanya carried a tarp that he would string up at night between trees.

I was intrigued. These Russian adventurers were tough! They had grown up during a period of great turmoil in their country, it turned out. Much had been scarce—food, clothing, fuel. Meanwhile, I had grown up with the choice of twenty different breakfast cereals on the grocery store shelves. There were three flavors of Cap'n Crunch alone! (My mother did not allow us to eat Cap'n Crunch, or any other sugared cereals. But I did dream about those three flavors often.)

That first evening we stopped in a field and began to set up camp. At this juncture, we Americans would have unpacked our waterproof lighters and our tiny propane stoves, most no bigger than our palm. But the Russians were in charge of the cooking supplies on this expedition. Ivan dropped his backpack, said something in Russian, reached in, and pulled out some matches. He reached in again. His hand reappeared, lugging a large pot.

A huge pot, actually.

Such a huge pot must be constructed of very light material, I thought to myself. But this was not a camping pot from America. This was a camping pot from Ivan's kitchen, and it was made of thick cast iron. I was flabbergasted. He

SHE SAID...

"I fell in love with the river, married it, and I don't plan no divorce."
—**Georgie White**, first woman to row the Grand Canyon, and by 1961 the most experienced guide on the river

had hauled that up the mountain on his back? As I was turning to exclaim to my friend Beth something along the lines of "He hauled that up the mountain on his back???" Ivan reached in again, and pulled out two cast-iron rods, which surely weighed as much as a cat. But that wasn't all. Between the rods was strung a thick metal wire. Finally he pulled out a thick metal hook.

There would be no tiny, featherweight camp stove. There would only be heavy cast-iron pots hung over roaring fires. This was the Russian way. Now I was curious about one other, more obvious thing. If there were so few supplies in Russia, how did Siberian rafters obtain rafts?

The answer is: They constructed them.

Hospital mattress covers, which had rubber coating that was water-resistant, were salvaged and packed in. At the riverside, branches were collected and carved into paddles. Other branches were fashioned into poles, which were then lashed together with steel wire or nylon cord to make a frame. The frame was then secured to two blown-up hospital-mattress-cover pontoons. Wow! A handsome, sturdy, two-hulled raft, called a cataraft, was now ready to take on the rapids.

Unfortunately, or probably fortunately, there would be no hand-constructed boats on our expedition. We would paddle fancy white-water boats, the best kayaks, and aluminum-framed, urethane-bladdered catarafts.

CATARAFT

The Sumulta had been run only a few times. That doesn't sound comforting to most people, but I'd paddled rivers that had never been run at all, and there was a big difference. If the river had been run at least once, you knew it was possible to run again. If it had never been run, you couldn't be sure.

We finally reached our destination. A helicopter had dropped off our boats, though Ivan could have carried each one on his back, I was sure. Soon we were on the river.

Those first few days the rapids were challenging, but to experienced paddlers like the ones on this expedition, they were not stomach-dropping, forehead-sweating, throat-tightening monsters. Then one morning a team meeting was called. Ahead of us was a rapid that demanded our fierce attention. To run all the boats through meant only the best would be guiding. This meant that some would forego the run and walk a side trail, while others would have to hike back upriver after a run and paddle another boat down.

I was by no means one of those expert guides, but I was a reliable paddler, so I volunteered to power a cataraft alongside Vlad, a young Russian who didn't speak a lick of English. This wouldn't matter, would it? There were only a few

SHE SAID...

"There's a difference between being careful and living in fear. The former will keep you alive, the latter will make you a bystander in people's lives."
—**Anna Fitzpatrick**, writer

words that, as the guide, he needed: Right turn, Left turn, Forward paddle, Back paddle. Just in case, we streamlined the commands to Right, Left, Forward, and Back and then made sure Vlad repeated them with the appropriate hand gestures to indicate he knew what they meant. I was given no words at all. My job was to obey what Vlad yelled. The words "Help," "Holy Cow," and "Take Me Back to Shore"? Not options.

Before the run, Beth took me aside. "You have to stay right as you near the bottom of the rapid," she hissed. "Understand? Stay right. If you don't, it's big, big trouble. There's a nasty drop on the left. You could die."

"Die" sounded a bit extreme. But Beth was a very experienced white-water athlete. She was also one of my best friends, and she knew I was prone to dumb mistakes. But I reminded her that Vlad was in the driver's seat. There wasn't a single dumb mistake I could make. He was guiding, and he'd run the rapid before. "Okay," Beth muttered. "Then he'll run it on the right." She glared at me but seemed appeased.

I straddled one pontoon, Vlad straddled the other, and we pushed off. I could feel the tension on shore, but I was relaxed. When your world is pared down to just four words, everything seems manageable, even a stomach-dropping, forehead-sweating, throat-tightening monster rapid like the one that had now grabbed our cataraft and was yanking it downstream.

The partnership began well. I paddled according to Vlad's commands. The cataraft darted and wheeled with the nimbleness of a soccer star. We sped by looming rocks, skirted whirling "holes," and powered through waves that reared like stallions and roared like lions. Everything was fine. I was grinning. Then I heard the command.

"Left!" Vlad shouted.

I swiveled my head from side to side. We were nearing the end of the rapid. Beth had specifically said that we had to stay right. Why was Vlad calling for a left turn? This couldn't be correct.

"Right?" I stammered, hoping that I would jog his memory.

"Left!" he countered, digging his paddle into the water, pulling us to the opposite bank.

"Right!" Now I dug in, too. From the shore I could hear someone yelling. It was Beth.

"Stay right! Stay right!" she screamed over the cascade of white water.

"Right!" I yelled again, continuing to paddle us that way. Now we were fighting each other. Both of us were strong. Both of us were desperate. Both of us had no way of negotiating with the other, beyond the words Right, Left, Forward, and Back. And at this point, paddling in opposing directions, neither of us was gaining much ground. It was clear: We were going to take an unknown middle course if we kept this up.

Beth's frantic cries became garbled as the river's roar increased. It didn't matter, I knew what she was yelling. Quickly I weighed the pros and cons. Wasn't it better to proceed as a coordinated team? Or should we keep warring in a cataraft that was now out of control? I wasn't sure. Suddenly I realized that just because I wasn't guiding it didn't mean I couldn't make a dumb mistake. What should I do?

SHE SAID...

"I don't just want to live the length of my life. I want to lead the breadth of it too."
—**Diane Ackerman**, wildlife naturalist, author

I reversed my paddle stroke. "Left!" I cried in agreement. "Left!"

I saw the six-foot drop a split second before the final command came in. Forward! shouted Vlad, like a general in battle. We charged over the waterfall, one pontoon catching momentarily on a rock. For a stomach-dropping, forehead-sweating, throat-tightening moment it seemed as if we would flip, but the rock let go and we were airborne, and then the water buried us in its white-foamed fury. As the cataraft ricocheted free, I gasped for air and looked wildly around, and Vlad yelled another command. We pivoted once, dropped again, jerked suddenly to one side, and then the rapid was over.

I didn't know the Russian words for What the Heck?! but it didn't matter. Vlad and I slapped paddles enthusiastically, and then disembarked, wordlessly forgiving each other for our mid-rapid spat. The rest of the expedition gathered around, congratulating us on a successful descent. Only Beth looked grim. She took me aside. "You didn't paddle to the right!" she said through clenched teeth. "I tried," I whined. I explained that Vlad was the guide and he had picked the opposite course. Without a real language between us, what else could I have done? Beth scowled. The only thing scarier than a monster rapid was Beth's wrath. But then she relented, and muttered the four vital English words to use after any encounter with feral water. "At least you're alive," she said.

I was not only alive, but I was a smidgen smarter than I had been just ten minutes earlier. I had learned a lesson I would never forget. Just because I wasn't the guide in charge, didn't mean I had no responsibilities. I should have learned the Russian words for Let's Talk About Our Route Together Before We Depart on this Stomach-dropping, Forehead-sweating, Throat-tightening Monster. Next time, I will.

DERRING-DO

USE TOOLS!

I used to think some people were naturally handy, and some people just weren't. But making, fixing, or dismantling something with tools is easily learned. Just ask my Siberian friends, who taught themselves to built catarafts with the most rudimentary of supplies!

The first tool you need is Confidence ("I can do this!"). The second tool is Curiosity (". . . but I wonder how to go about it.") Also, grab some Patience, if you can find it. Now summon an Adult. She has the tools in her basement (or the money to buy them), and she can help instruct on their proper use, since I can't be there in person.

Try this: Gather up tools and get to work using them!

Hammer—Hammer five nails into a board. You might have to hold the hammer close to the head. That's fine! Now remove the nails, using the prying end.

Screwdriver—Screw five screws into a piece of wood. You may have to hammer a small hole first, and set the screw in. NOTE: There are two kinds of screwdrivers. A flathead screwdriver is used for screws with one groove on the head. A Phillips screwdriver is used for screws with criss-cross grooves on the head. Find and use both!

Claw bar (also known as a pry bar)—Insert the flat head under a piece of wood that is nailed down. Push down on the handle, and watch the wood begin to separate from its companion. Stop, reposition the claw bar deeper into the gap, and begin again. (Please do not pry off the wall of your house, or your parents' bed. Hammer two pieces of wood together and use that!)

Drill—Insert five screws into a piece of wood with a drill! Now switch the direction lever and remove the five screws.

DERRING-DO
MAPS

Yes, yes, I've heard it too—use global positioning system (GPS) devices to navigate. But paper maps are awesome. They don't use batteries or need cell tower reception. Carry them as backup! There are many kinds of maps. A street map emphasizes roads, highways, and streets. A nautical chart is more concerned with water depth, coastlines, and islands. Maps for pilots concentrate on landmarks that can be seen from the air, such as tall electrical towers, railways, and highways. A topographical map describes landscape by using lines that get closer together as the terrain gets steeper, and farther apart as the terrain levels out.

Try this: Find a map for your location (a map of your hometown, for instance, or if you're outside, a trail map). Look first at its key (usually found in a box in one corner of the map). Learn the symbols! Now you can decipher your map. Orient your map so it corresponds to where you are facing. You can do this by picking landmarks and comparing them to the map, or with a compass. (Maps are drawn so north is up, south is down, west is left, and east is right.)

Try this: Pick a place on your map, close by. Mark it on your map with a circle. You're ready: Walk or bike to the circled area!

JOURNAL THIS!

Here's another (of the many) cool things about adventures. It doesn't matter what you look like! In an adventure, it only matters who you are. Are you calm, courteous, physically fit, thoughtful, observant, humorous, open-minded, resilient, and team-oriented? Great! Do you know how to whittle, pitch a tent, fix a bike tire? Awesome!

Write down four qualities you possess that would really rock in an adventure, and why. Go!

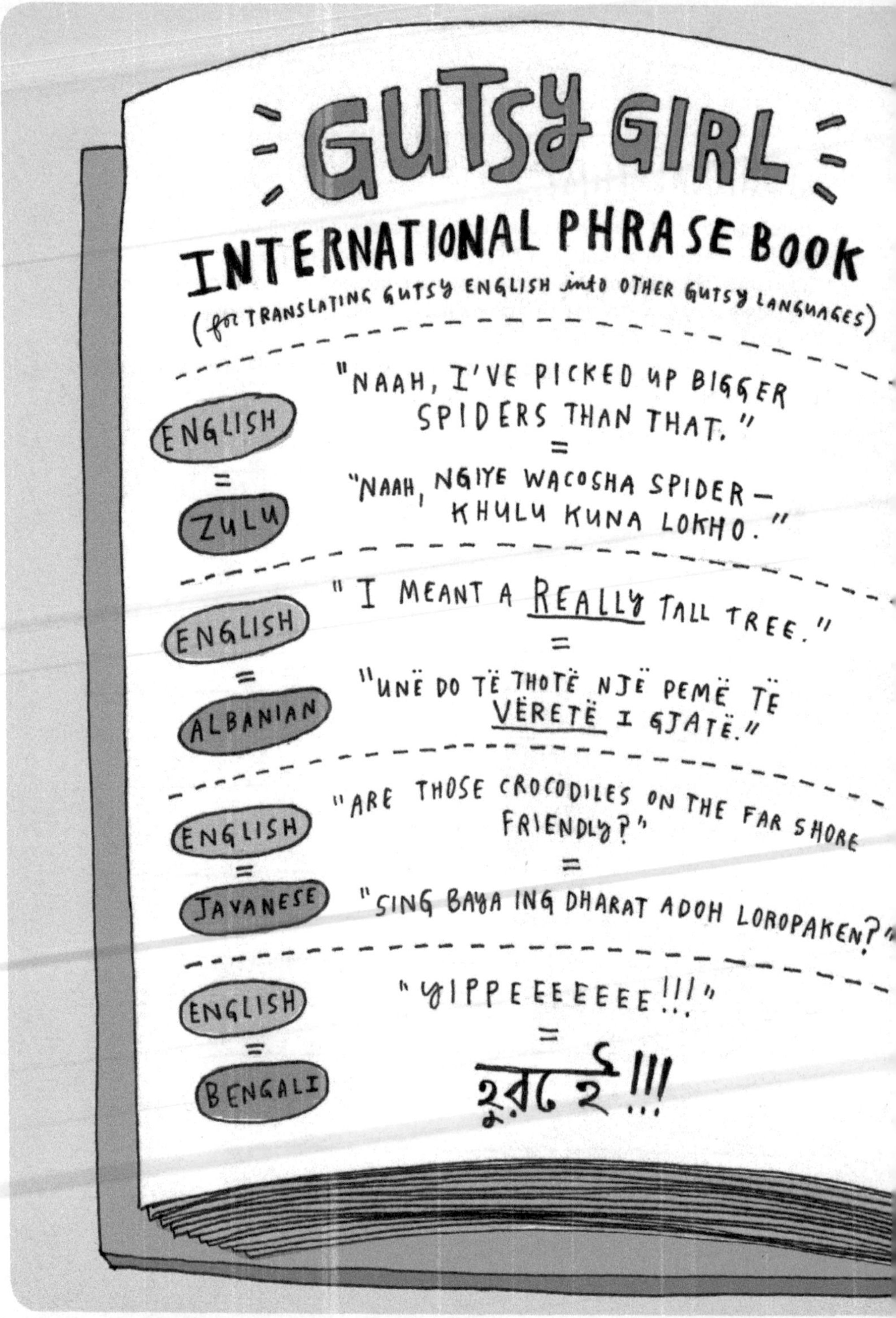

(con't.)

ENGLISH
=
NORWEGIAN

"IS THAT AN ICEBERG AHEAD?"
=
"ER DET ET ISFJELL FREMOVER?"

ENGLISH
=
GERMAN

"WHO BROUGHT SNACKS?!"
=
"WER BRACHTE SNACKS?!"

ENGLISH
=
HAITIAN

"WE DON'T SPEAK 'SCARDEY CAT' HERE."
=
"NOU PA PALE 'SCAREDY CAT' ISIT LA."

ENGLISH
=
MAORI

"IS THAT A BEAR OR JUST A TREE THAT APPEARS to BE RUNNING TOWARD US?!"
=
"E TEA PEA TE RAKAU TIKA RANEI E PUTA KI TE RERE KI A TAATOU?!"

ENGLISH *
=
SIGN LANGUAGE

"LET'S GO!" =

* SPOKEN

CHAPTER 9

PLAN WELL, THEN EXPECT THE UNEXPECTED

THE SKY WAS thick with rain clouds. It was dusk. We didn't have much time before nightfall. I paddled my sea kayak and craned my neck toward shore at the same time. We needed to pull over and camp. But there were only soaring cliffs on one side of us, and the darkening Adriatic Sea on the other.

I called to my two companions in sea kayaks nearby. "Didn't we ask Zjelko if there was camping, and he said yes?"

"We asked him if we were allowed to camp," Sue called back. "We failed to ask him if it was possible."

Beth shook her head and let out a laugh.

We thought we'd planned this expedition to Croatia well. We'd studied the maps. We'd scoured the Internet (which was new, and didn't have much valuable information at that time). We'd contacted the one and only adventure outfitter in the whole country. We'd traveled to the small village of Zaton, where that adventure outfitter resided, rented the sea kayaks, and picked the owner's brain about possible routes. The owner, a man named Zjelko, had pointed out the islands we might want to see, then warned us of the mistral winds. They howled from early morning onward this time of year, he told us. Our faces fell. Mistrals hadn't been mentioned when we'd first contacted him about this trip. But we'd flown all the way here, and committed two weeks to our adventure. Miraculously, the winds were quiet on our departure day. Zjelko declared us lucky, and waved us off.

But right now, as dusk settled and storm clouds roiled above us, we didn't feel lucky. We felt stupid. We had assumed that the words "island" and "sea" naturally led to the word "beach." Miles from the mainland, we'd realized: The coast of this island was steep-walled and rocky. Our plans to camp each night were evaporating before our eyes. We would have to find pensiones and sleep in beds. Truthfully, that sounded kind of nice. But these islands were sparsely populated. Right now there was no town in sight. According to the map, there was no town for hours.

GIRL HERO!

 One day **Roz Savage** wrote herself two obituaries: the first for the person she actually was and the second for the person she wanted to be. Realizing the two obituaries differed mightily, she gave up her job as a management consultant, sold her house, and embarked on a life of adventure. She is best known for being the first woman to row alone across the Atlantic, Pacific, and Indian oceans.

A raindrop hit my nose.

"It's raining," shouted Beth. Sometimes stating the obvious was better than looking at our deepening silhouettes or hearing the smack of our paddles in the draining light.

"Why didn't Zjelko tell us about this?" I whined. But we knew why. He was the owner of the only sea kayaks in the country, but he had never paddled to this island, or to the ones we were heading for. No one had. We were the first sea kayakers to attempt this multi-day expedition. Sailboats were common, but the sailors we had talked to had said nothing about the lack of level ground either. We realized, belatedly, that sailors don't eye islands for campsites; they sleep on their boats. Everyone seemed to think that camping was everywhere, because they'd never actually needed to camp.

We were thrilled to be the first to sea kayak these islands. But when you're the first, all the planning in the world can quickly become irrelevant. When you're the first, there are a lot of unknowns. "Keep looking," Sue shouted back. Our three kayaks picked up speed.

GIRL HEROES!

In 1966 **Roberta Gibb** became the first woman to run the Boston Marathon. At the time women were barred from this and many other long-distance events, under the pretext that their bodies were too frail, so Bobbi ran unofficially. There were 415 (male) entrants that year; Bobbi finished ahead of 290 of them.

The first woman to race officially in the 26.2-mile Boston Marathon was twenty-year-old **Kathrine Switzer**, who signed up for the race in 1967 as K.V. Switzer. At mile two, race officials spotted Kathrine and tried to pull her from the course, but they were fended off by her teammates from the Syracuse University track team. "I'm going to finish this race on my hands and knees if I have to, because no one believes I can do this," she said. She crossed the finish line—on her feet!—and (along with Bobbi) upended the world's view of female endurance.

Two days earlier, Zjelko had waved us good-bye, looking pleased. He had been trying to get his company off the ground for a few years, but Croatia, still recovering from a five-year war, didn't seem to understand the outdoor adventure travel industry. The government wasn't giving him the required permits. The young locals wouldn't sign up as guides, because they didn't view adventure travel as a real career. Now three American women were renting his kayaks. We were the beginning, he hoped.

Zjelko didn't seem to doubt our ability to complete our eight-day expedition, but everyone else did. We crossed to the first island, paddled into its ancient port town, weaved among the sailboats and fishing craft, and pulled our boats onto the rocky shore (this should have been our first clue that the terrain was not as we had thought). Friendly locals stared at the sea kayaks, stared at us, then asked in practiced English which sailboat moored out there was ours.

"We didn't come from a sailboat. We came from there," we answered, and pointed to the distant mainland. They looked at us with disbelief. "So dangerous!" one of the men tutted.

"Not really," said Beth, sweetly, while Sue and I nodded. We didn't explain that Beth had river-kayaked huge white water around the world, or that Sue had once been on the U.S. National Whitewater Kayaking team. We didn't explain that paddling across smooth ocean on a sunny day was our idea of relaxation. The language barrier seemed too great for that. Besides, we liked striking a small, quiet blow for girl power, in a place that seemed to need it.

We ate at a busy sidewalk restaurant and watched people gambol by. Beth

---

SHE SAID...

"I used to believe money could buy you happiness . . . now I've found that not having a lot of stuff gives me incredible freedom." —**Roz Savage**, ocean rower, who gave up a well-paying career, a big house, and a nice car for a simpler life

---

ordered fish. "We're by the sea," she said, "so it's bound to be excellent." It was excellent, so Beth ordered another. Then she ordered another. She ate three fish that night.

What we didn't know was that the Adriatic Sea had been dangerously overfished. There were only a few wild species left. These were considered a rare delicacy. Beth ordered fish, but it was just like ordering gold. We thought we'd be paying ten dollars each for our meals. Beth paid eighty.

We were sobered by the sudden expense, but we were even more sobered by what it represented. Could it be that the crystalline waters we'd paddled on were almost lifeless? This made us sad. The islands seemed wild, the ocean vibrant. But humans had made a mess here after all.

Our plan for that first night was to paddle out of town and camp. Instead we finished our infamous fish dinner and wandered through narrow streets gazing at the sea views, Then we pitched our tents in a hidden corner of the rocky marina. Before sleep we gathered together and gazed at the map. We'd tried to get more information from the locals about their island, but they were too aghast to be of much help. "That's so dangerous," each said, when we explained we were circumnavigating Korcula. Then what about the next island, we'd ask. They shook their head in wonder. "The next island!" they would lament. "You are crazy girls!"

So we stared at the map ourselves. "Look, there are no towns on that side,"

SHE SAID...

"I sucked." —**Ishita Malaviya**, India's first female to ever surf, now a sponsored pro who owns her own surf shop, on her first few sessions in the water

GIRL HERO!

Ten-year-old **Willow McConochie** of Maine spends much of her free time outdoors. She climbs trees, hikes, and cross-country skis. She camps in all seasons, even in the mid-winter snow! She also helps her dad set up their "game camera," which is tied to a tree, baited with hot dogs, then left to shoot photos of the wildlife that comes nosing around. The next day Willow and her father ski or hike back into the woods to check who has visited the night before. The game camera has caught owls, coyotes, and foxes, and this winter a fisher was photographed—an animal that Willow describes as almost the size of her dog Mabel, really black, with long claws and a love of eating chickens.

---

said Beth, tracing her finger to the northern tip. "It'll be perfect camping."

But now here we were, a day later, and it wasn't perfect camping, not by a long shot. Cliffs and more cliffs, is all we saw. We downgraded our hopes. We didn't need a sandy beach! Any flat spot would do. But even a flat spot was nowhere to be found.

We pondered our options, which by now were few. Number one: We could put on our headlamps and keep paddling. Number two: A long, fine beach of white sand could suddenly appear around the corner and we would camp safely for the night. But this was unlikely, and we needed other options. Number three: We could put on our headlamps and keep paddling.

I had paddled at night before, but only under a full moon. Tonight would be overcast at best, raining at worst. Still, how bad could it be? We might have to drift farther out to sea to avoid rocks. We might be uncomfortable (we would definitely be uncomfortable). We might be frightened by the pitch black and our inability to navigate. But we wouldn't die. Sometimes just knowing this fact is enough to gather the courage you need.

"We'll eat from the snack bags," Sue said brightly. "No expensive fish meal tonight."

The waters hadn't been completely bereft of wildlife, it turned out. That day, dolphins had shot out of the water in bright spinning arcs. A whale had breached over and over, as if welcoming us to her waters. To add to the magic, the mistral winds had once again held off. The waters sparkled green, the cliffs soared above us, and every now and then an old church, perched high on the hill, long abandoned, came into sight. We ooh-ed and ahh-ed. We marveled that no one had sea kayaked these waters before. We gloated that we were the first. "Girl Power!" we shouted happily to each other.

The rain had stopped, for now. The last of the day seeped away. Suddenly Beth whistled, and flapped her paddle to the cliffs. Sue and I squinted in the gray light. There it was, a small inlet, just big enough for three kayaks, and above that a black ledge of some sort. If we could secure our kayaks, then climb onto the ledge, there was a chance we'd sleep tonight. It looked

SHE SAID...

"It would be the chili that my mom makes—we carry it in and then defrost it. And s'mores." —**Willow McConochie**, ten, describing her favorite camping meals

GIRL HERO!

Surfing is called the sport of kings, but it was actually the sport of queens and princesses, too. Hawaiian royalty rode boards as long as sixteen feet made of wood from the wiliwili tree. When the first missionaries landed on the islands, they were shocked to see Hawaiian women riding waves (they were shocked to see men, too, as they'd never seen surfing before.) **Princess Ka'iulani**, born in 1875, was a skilled surfer and swimmer.

---

improbable. But it was possible. Possible was what we needed.

We tied our kayaks to thick bushes that grew out from the rock. Knee deep in water, clinging to the bushes ourselves, we surveyed the rock that jutted into the sea; a large piece of the cliff must have broken off thousands of years ago and landed on this spot, just for us. Up we climbed. The surface was pitted and uneven—volcanic rock, we guessed. Great for climbing, not so great for sleeping. But we were in no position to be picky. At the top we surveyed our choices. The rock wasn't flat by any means, but it would do.

"Last Minute Ledge!" I yipped with glee. (One of the compulsions that accompany being the first at something is that you name the places you find.)

We each found spots on which to throw our sleeping bags. There wasn't enough room for tents, so we unpacked tarps and lay under them, which was smart, because it rained that night. By morning I was wet and cold. The rain had stopped hours before but what remained had pooled in the flatter areas, so I had slept in a puddle. But our kayaks were still there, safely tied up. We had gotten uneven sleep, but it was sleep just the same. We staggered about, stiff and tired and a little grumpy. Then Beth stopped, stared at the sea, and looked back at Sue and me.

"Another day with no mistrals," she smiled. "We sure are lucky!"

For the rest of the trip we slept in beds, in towns. Miraculously, the mistrals held off. Still, we were met everywhere with wide eyes and shocked hand gestures. "You girls, in kayak, island to island?"

"Yep," we'd answer, shrugging and smiling.

"Dangerous!" they'd yelp.

"Nope," we'd say. Then, remembering Last Minute Ledge, we'd amend ourselves. "Not dangerous. But sometimes . . . a little unexpected."

DERRING-DO
LOST IN THE WILD!

Experts say that if you're lost it's best to stay put and wait for rescue. One reason is that people often walk in circles, wasting valuable energy, confusing rescuers, and accomplishing nothing. But if you absolutely can't stay put (running out of chocolate does not count as a reason you can't stay put) and you know there are roads or trails nearby, navigate using landmarks to walk in a straight line.

Try this: Pick a prominent landmark, such as a tree, and then pick one behind that, to form a straight line from you. Walk to the first landmark. Now pick another landmark beyond your second landmark, also in a straight line. Continue until you reach a road. NOTE: Do not pick large moose, bears, or clouds as landmarks. Or anything else that might move.

DERRING-DO

PLAN AN ADVENTURE!

Adventures often involve travel to parts unknown to you (this could be as far away as Croatia, or as close as the park in the next town). Planning a trip takes practice.

Try this: Get out a globe. Find Croatia. See where it is in relation to the rest of the world. Spin the globe a few times, and find another country you're curious about. Look up its history. Look up its sights. Now write down your ideal adventure itinerary! What town/mountain/river would you first visit, and what would you do there? Where would you go next?

JOURNAL THIS!

When it comes to chocolate, we all know: We want it. A cute kitten in our lap? Ditto. More attention from our BFF? Of course! But sometimes it can be hard to ask! We're afraid that our teammates, our friends, or that cool older kid will think we're needy, silly, or just plain dumb. But here's the truth: Your needs matter. Learn to ask for what you want!

Write down four things you want that a person can grant if asked. Is it a bigger allowance? A chance to visit the new national park nearby? Inclusion at a lunch table? Now write down the name of the person you would have to ask and the sentence you need to say in order to obtain it.

PLAN YOUR ADVENTURE!

WHERE DO I WANT to GO? _____
_____

WHO WILL BE MY ADVENTURE BUDDY/BUDDIES?
_____
_____

WILL I KAYAK, HIKE, BIKE, RAFT, MOUNTAINEER, SKATEBOARD, UNICYCLE, OR WALK? _____
_____ OR OTHER? _____

HOW MUCH TIME DO I HAVE for THIS ADVENTURE?
_____

WHAT MAPS DO I NEED of THIS REGION (TOPOGRAPHIC? STREET?) AND HOW DETAILED MUST THEY BE? _____
_____

WHAT ARE THE CHARACTERISTICS of THE LANDSCAPE I'M TRAVELING to? _____
_____

WHAT ARE SOME CHARACTERISTICS of THE PEOPLE, CULTURE, RELIGIONS THERE? _____
_____

WHAT IS THE HISTORY of THIS COUNTRY/REGION/ NEW TOWN/LOCAL PARK? _____
_____
_____

IS THERE SEASONAL WEATHER to CONSIDER? _____
DO I HAVE to GET SHOTS? _____ IF I HAVE to GET SHOTS, DO I STILL WANT to GO? (YES, YOU DO!)
HOW MUCH MONEY WILL THIS COST? _____
_____

HOW CAN I SAVE UP for THIS? _____
_____
_____

WHAT EQUIPMENT SHOULD I BRING and WHAT EQUIP- MENT CAN I PICK UP THERE? _____
_____
_____
_____

WILL MY PARENTS SAY YES? _____
IF NOT, HOW CAN I GET THEM to SAY YES?
_____
_____

CHAPTER 10

WHERE THERE'S SMOKE, THERE'S FIRE,
AND SOMETIMES KITTENS

THE FIRST DOG I ever rescued bit me. I held on, so he dropped two poops onto the sleeve of my fire coat. I couldn't blame him: I was just the latest bummer in what had been a very bad doggy day. There had been flames, there had been smoke, there had been the shouts of strange people. With an axe at my side, and an air mask on my face, I was as scary as the rest. But I held him tightly and, whispering promises of dog bones and hugs, I carried him to fresh air. The owner rushed at us, arms outstretched, crying.

This was a fairly typical workday for me. I was a San Francisco firefighter, part of a crew called Rescue 2. Our job was to search for victims in fires, and sometimes those victims were dogs who pooped on our fire coats.

When my career began in 1989 there were barely any female firefighters, in the whole wide world. In the San Francisco Fire Department, for instance, I was the fifteenth woman hired. That may sound like a lot, until you realize that there were one thousand five hundred men.

This meant that I was the only female firefighter on my shift. Sometimes I was the only female firefighter the other men had ever seen! I loved the job and I respected many of my coworkers but, let's face it, it's tough to be different. As the only woman, I was left out of the jokes. I was excluded from the easy camaraderie. I often didn't understand the social rules. For the most part the ostracization wasn't purposeful. It was like joining a class halfway through school. The friend groups are set. You're not invited in. I was that kid with weird hair and crazy clothes who couldn't find someone to eat with at lunch.

Firefighting was full of adventure and excitement, but it was also difficult, those first years. People had a lot of questions. Were women strong enough? Were women brave enough? I was watched very carefully. Any mistake would

GIRL HERO!

 Lea Ann Parsley became the State of Ohio Firefighter of the Year in 1999 after she and another firefighter pulled a disabled teenager from her burning home. Upon hearing that the girl's mother was still inside, Lea Ann alerted her officer, then crawled back into the smoke with her crew. As conditions worsened, Lea Ann located the unconscious woman and dragged her toward a window. With help from a fellow firefighter, Lea Ann hauled the woman onto her lap and tumbled backward out the window "like a scuba diver flopping off the side of a boat." Holy cow! As if that weren't enough derring-do, Lea Ann was also a top-notch skeleton athlete at the time. She won a silver medal at the 2002 Olympic games!

GIRL HEROES!

In 1913, **Hallie Daggett** become the first female fire lookout hired by the U.S. Forest Service. She hiked three hours up Klamath Peak to the Eddy Gulch fire tower and lived there by herself for many months, spotting smoke and alerting fire crews (depending on the tower this was done using carrier pigeons, telephone, or "heliographs"—mirrored devices that used sunlight to flash Morse code across great distances). To the surprise of many, Hallie was not afraid, or desperately lonely; she relished the job and signed up for the next fourteen fire seasons. Lookout **Nancy Hood** has worked over fifty-five straight fire seasons—more than anyone else ever in the U.S.!

not just reflect on me, it would reflect on all women, and each female firefighter knew it. Some of the men were mean in ways that were so dumb and embarrassing for them it isn't worth mentioning here. But many were decent and respectful, even if they, too, had doubts about female firefighters. Soon three of us women had joined the biggest station in the city, on the rig that responded to the most fires, called Rescue 2. Another woman joined Rescue 1. Still others chose to work on busy fire engines or fire trucks (NOTE: The engines hold the water, the trucks carry the ladders!). We trained hard off duty—running for miles, lifting heavy weights. Soon some of us were more experienced than those who criticized us!

WHAT IT LOOKS LIKE IN A FIRE

Join me now at a fairly typical fire. That's me, crawling down a hallway. I'm hauling hose, but you can't see me because the smoke is so thick. I can't see me, either—not my hand in front of my face, not the beam of the flashlight on my shoulder, not the floor beneath me. My partner, Victor, is behind me, and he keeps bumping into me, but that's okay, because I keep bumping into

Frank, who in turn must be bumping into Andy, who is at the front of the line and is most certainly bumping into walls. This is how it goes in what we called "a really good fire," which to most people actually means "a really bad fire"—terrible visibility, a lot of clambering around, and air that seems made of molten lava stinging your ears.

At this particular fire, none of the other crews had found the flames yet, and conditions were worsening, which was why the chief sent the four of us into this hallway. Rescue 2 was a specialized unit, used mostly for rescues, but if someone was going to give us a hose and shout "Get in there and find the fire!" we were happy to do it.

It was getting hotter. For most people, hotter meant "turn around, run away!" But we were San Francisco firefighters. Hotter meant we were on the right track. We advanced down the hallway. Every now and then Andy opened up the nozzle to cool the air. The heated water would fall back on us and seep into our Nomex fire pants. But I didn't notice any pain (later, I would find small spots of second-degree burns). I was too intent on our mission: Find the fire.

We should have sensed something was wrong. It was too dark, too hot. The fire was still not in sight—even in this thick smoke, flames would be visible first as flashes, then as we got closer, we would see long tendrils that slithered and danced like snakes. Finally it would appear, huge, savage, roaring, an orange beast at full charge—but not today. Today it was eerily quiet.

And then the air exploded. We were thrown backward. There was immense light and maybe noise, too, but I can't remember much. Moments later I was on my knees in the garage, dazed, looking around. The air was cool, visibility

SHE SAID...

"You gain strength, courage, and confidence by every experience in which you really stop to look fear in the face." —First Lady **Eleanor Roosevelt**

SHE SAID...

"Dudley went to the left and I went to the right . . . It was getting much harder to see but finally, as I reached underneath a desk, I grabbed hold of a woman's arm. I pulled as hard as I could and she slid out along the floor." —**Lea Ann Parsley**, decorated firefighter and silver medal Olympian, describing the rescue of an unconscious woman in a house fire

was back. Why were we here? Weren't we just there? Frank grabbed my shoulder, then Andy's.

"Are you okay!? Are you okay!??" he yelled at each of us through his air mask. "Yes! Yes!" Andy and I yelled back.

Then Frank shouted, "Where's Victor?"

Victor? Victor! I swiveled my head around frantically. Victor wasn't in the garage. That meant he was in the hallway, that hallway, the one from which we had just been thrown like whiffle balls. Had he survived?

Frank was already jettisoning himself toward the door, back the way we had come. I tried to follow. But my arms and legs felt like molasses. My mind was screaming "Hold it, you're going back in there?? Are you crazy? We were almost killed!" and for the first time in my life as a firefighter, I hesitated.

Hesitated!

I was—dare I say it—afraid.

But in the next second I knew this: Frank was afraid, too. But fear wasn't going to stop him. Why should it? A member of our crew was in danger. Fear was understandable, but right now it wasn't helpful. It couldn't dictate our actions. I plunged into the corridor behind Frank. It was dark. It was hot. And we ran right into Victor. He was unhurt. He had scrambled into a room adjacent to the garage.

"Why were you so worried?" he scoffed, trying to make light of what we knew had been a narrow escape for all of us.

We had survived one of the most deadly of fire behaviors—a "flashover."

A flashover occurs when temperatures from the fire get so hot—up to 1200 degrees—that nearby objects simultaneously ignite. Even the particles in the air explode! We were lucky—the flashover hadn't occurred in the hallway, just nearby. If it had occurred in the hallway, I wouldn't be here to tell the tale.

That day I felt a fear I had never before experienced. And fear, I learned, could paralyze me. Luckily I could also un-paralyze myself. Fear was an emotion I didn't have to buckle under. It was about putting action and courage first and foremost.

Even afraid, I could crawl into burning hallways.

Firefighting was not always death-defying. One day my crew arrived on the scene too late for any action. It had been a small fire, confined to one room; an engine crew had already extinguished it. We were disappointed—firefighters love fighting fires, but not in a weird way, don't worry. We love fighting fires for the excitement. We love fighting fires for the joy of stopping further destruction. In other words, we don't want a fire to happen, but if there is going to be one, we'd like to be there.

But that day we were out of luck. We jumped from the rig anyway, and walked toward the chief for instructions. I could still see smoke wafting from the window several stories up, but clearly the flames were out. Then something caught my eye. A small black object, on the ledge outside the smoking window. I squinted. Was it alive? Yes, it was.

I took the stairs two at a time. I rushed past the crew in the apartment. I

SHE SAID...

"You practice your exits, your landings, and everything else so many times, that when you finally get up into the airplane, you're really more focused on 'Am I going to do this right?' rather than, 'Oh my God, I'm about to jump out of a plane.'"
—Wildland firefighter **Ramona Atherton**, on her training as a smoke jumper. Smoke jumpers parachute from planes into the wilderness to fight forest fires.

asked someone to grab my coat, then I leaned as far as I could out the window. There she was, just within arm's reach: a tiny, mewling black kitten. "Hello," I said in my most soothing voice.

Below a crowd of gawkers milled like ants, but I didn't allow myself to look down. I extended my arm slowly. I tried to communicate pure thoughts of animal love. I murmured nonsensical assurances. I hoped for a miracle. And the miracle happened. The kitten didn't run, as kittens are wont to do when strangers approach. I grabbed, latching on to her tiny scruff, and pulled her back into the apartment. She was shivering, so I dropped her into my coat. I held her next to my heart. "You're okay," I told her, "you're okay," and together we headed for the stairs.

DERRING-DO

GET OUT OF YOUR COMFORT ZONE!

What is a Comfort Zone? It sounds like a warm room with lots of pillows, kittens, waterbeds, and candy. It's not (though if you know of such a room, direct me to it immediately). Instead it refers to the areas in your life that feel easy and seamless to you. We all love comfort zones, because it's nice to feel relaxed, and it's nice to be really good at something. But it's important to challenge yourself, too! So get out of your room of pillows, kittens, waterbeds, and candy. How? Learn something new, get better at something you already know, or push yourself to overcome a fear.

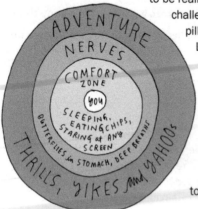

Try this: Make a vow with yourself to get out of your comfort zone once a week or more. This may mean raising your hand in class, picking up an earwig, or dancing in public. Keep a list of your efforts! Better yet, pick an Adventure Buddy, and do this together.

DERRING-DO
MAKE A COMPASS

There's an easy way make sure you don't get lost. Learn to make a compass! Okay, this doesn't work inside smoky buildings. But it's great for hiking in the great outdoors!

Try this: Find a field or open yard on a sunny day. Put a tall (about three-foot) stick into the ground. Make sure it stands straight. Place a marker (rock, leaf, even a piece of pie, but NOT ice cream) where the shadow of the stick ends. After anywhere from fifteen minutes to one hour, place another marker at the end of the new shadow. Now step between the stick and the two markers, with your big toe on the first marker and the other big toe on the second marker. You are facing North! From here it is easy to figure out East, West, and South.

JOURNAL THIS!

When was the last time you got out of your comfort zone? How did it make you feel? (See chart on page 26!) What is the next comfort zone challenge you will conquer? Go!

EPILOGUE

USUALLY WHEN A book ends, like this one has, the author types THE END with a flourish. But it occurred to me that while the words herein are over, your own tales of ridiculous adventure are just beginning. As you embark on a grand journey of leadership, bravery, humor, intermittent failures, repeated successes, serial resilience, sporadic embarassments, exhilaration, connection, and utmost joy, it's only fitting that I omit the usual words THE END. Instead I leave you, Gutsy Girl, with:

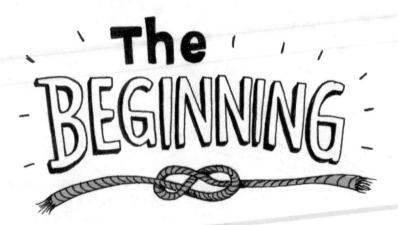

GO FORTH.

ACKNOWLEDGMENTS

QUITE A FEW gutsy girls were consulted during the writing of this book. Many, many thanks to Audrey Duane, Hannah Duane, and Alessia Rypins Gressi. The Mother–Daughter Book Club at the West Portal branch of the San Francisco Public Library also read the manuscript and over cookies and juice gave critical insight and much encouragement. Led by fearless librarian Liesel Harris-Boundy, these gutsy advisors were Etta Thornton and her mother, Jennifer Thornton; Fiorella Martin and her mother, Claudia Martin; Masey Milham and her mother, Yvonne Milham; Sadie Rawlings-Fein and her mother, Shelli Fein; Anastasia Dang, and Emily Lem. Thank you. This book is infinitely better because of your collective wisdom.

Thanks also to Liz Weil, Kate Schatz, Teresha Freckleton-Petite, Peggy Orenstein, Sophia Raday, India McConochie, librarian Jennifer Ambrulevich, and Simone Marean of Girls Leadership. Ongoing thanks to my agent, Charlotte Sheedy, and my editor, Nancy Miller, for their unwavering faith and guidance, and to Lea Beresford for handling all the logistics with such care. A shout-out to my hardworking pals at the San Francisco Writers' Grotto and especially to Diana Kapp, who said to me at our lunch table one day, "You must write a book for girls about your adventures. They need to hear them." Without her, *The Gutsy Girl* would not exist. Thanks also to my surf buddy and fellow Grotto writer Rodes Fishburne for his insight and advice. Thanks to my twin, Alexandra Paul, and to my mom, Sarah Paul, who read early versions and laughed in all the right places. To my partner, the illustrator Wendy MacNaughton: you put your heart into this book for me, and I'm so grateful.

Thanks to the gutsy girls and guys who have accompanied me on my adventures over the years but who did not make it into the book. It just means that nothing went terribly wrong. You are all an inspiration.